LEARNING FOR SUCCESS

SKILLS AND STRATEGIES FOR CANADIAN STUDENTS

Joan FLEET
Fiona GOODCHILD
Richard ZAJCHOWSKI

D1314909

HBJ

Harcourt Brace Jovanovich
Toronto Orlando San Diego London Sydney

Canadian Cataloguing in Publication Data

Fleet, Joan, 1939-
  Learning for Success

ISBN 0-7747-3143-5

1. Study, Method of. I. Goodchild, Fiona, 1943-
II. Zajchowski, Richard. III. Title.

LB1049.F53 1989   378′.170281   C89-094970-0

Publisher: **David Dimmell**
Acquisitions Editor: **Heather McWhinney**
Developmental Editor: **Greame Whitley**
Publishing Services Manager: **Karen Eakin**
Cover and Design: **Jack Steiner Graphic Design**
Cover Illustration: **Peter Nagy**
Interior Illustrations: **Nancy Somerville**
Typesetting and Assembly: **SCiTEX Services**
Printed in Canada

 2 3 4 5   94 93 92 91 90

CONTENTS IN BRIEF

CONTENTS

A NOTE TO STUDENTS

Most students come to college or university as natural learners, that is they have never given much thought to how they learn — they just do it and do it quite well. You may be one such student and you may find that the college or university experience puts heavier demands on your learning than ever before. It is like moving up to the big leagues — everything is faster and more challenging. Natural ability can still carry you a long way but you will almost certainly do better if you get some good coaching. This book gives good coaching advice, with its focus on how to be a better student. Specifically this book is for you.

A NOTE TO INSTRUCTORS AND COUNSELLORS

Educators are stressing more and more that "Learning to Learn" is as important as is learning the content knowledge of a course. Researchers suggest that students' awareness of how they study, as well as the methods they choose to use, are both critical factors in successful learning. Although this book addresses the learning challenges facing college and university students, it is also appropriate to self-directed learning at the secondary school level. We have had many discussions with instructors and counsellors at all levels within the school system about the learning strategies their students find useful, and there is no doubt that early strategy training in schools can establish valuable general attitudes and approaches to study.

LOOK OUT FOR ADDITIONAL TITLES!

A companion volume to this book is *FIT TO PRINT: A Canadian Student's Guide to Essay Writing* by Joanne Buckley. Watch out for other books in this series, dealing with academic issues and student learning, which will be appearing in the future.

THE GOALS OF THIS BOOK ARE TO:

- raise awareness of, and interest in, the learning process generally.

- increase each student's awareness of herself/himself as a learner.

- introduce specific strategies for more effective learning.

- suggest that each student controls many of the factors affecting her/his own successful academic performance.

- stimulate interest in research on the part of professionals on strategies for effective learning.

We would like to acknowledge the contribution of all those students, faculty, and staff at **The University of Western Ontario** who have participated with us in a continuing joint learning venture. Without their interest and support this project would not have been possible. In particular we would like to thank our colleagues in **Counselling and Career Development Services** and Maria Lavdas of SciTEX **Services** within the Department of Statistical and Actuarial Sciences for all her interest and expertise. We would also like to thank David Dimmell, publisher, Heather McWhinney, Acquisitions Editor and Karen Eakin, Publishing Services Manager at **Harcourt Brace Jovanovich Canada**.

STRATEGY CHECKLIST

Before you read this book it will be useful for you to assess some of your current learning strategies. Of course there are many others, but these may give you a flavour of some you already use or wish to use.

For each strategy either check **YES** (I usually/often do this) or check **NO** (I seldom / never do this).

A. IMMEDIATE STUDY ENVIRONMENT

Do you give attention to:
                                                    YES   NO

1. Selecting a study location relatively free of distractions?
2. Selecting a study location with adequate light and ventilation?
3. Having on hand useful materials such as paper, stapler, calculator, ruler?
4. Setting up a system to organize all notes and handouts for each course, so you can quickly locate essential materials such as old tests?
5. Planning your time so that you can give a reasonable amount of time to each course?

B. CAMPUS RESOURCES

Have you found:

1. A few colleagues with whom you can consult in each course you are taking?
2. When and what kind of assistance is available from your instructor or tutorial leader?
3. The help centres for any of your courses?
4. Ways of preparing questions so that your times with a resource person are as useful as possible?
5. Any old exams that are available (e.g., in library) and the way to get them?
6. Any alternate textbooks and reference material which may be helpful when you have difficulties?
7. A method of keeping track of material and information on bulletin boards (e.g., sample tests, solutions)?
8. Where and what kind of assistance is available at the Counselling Centre, Health Services, and other Student Services agencies?

C. PERSONAL HEALTH AND EFFECTIVENESS

Do you maintain: YES   NO

1. A regular sleep pattern (7–9 hours/night)?
2. A daily balanced diet?
3. A reasonable amount of regular exercise?

Do you make time for:

4. A few hours a week for your own enjoyment?
5. Getting away for a while either physically or mentally when problems or pressures arise?
6. Finding and talking to people to whom you can turn when you encounter difficulties?
7. Practising relaxation so that you can calm down if necessary?
8. Meeting other students who want to do well at school?
9. Focussing on the needs of others around you?

D. INTERNAL MENTAL PROCESSING

Do you consciously plan to:

1. Reduce information by listening and reading for key ideas?
2. Keep track of the overall structure of the information by tracking themes using headings?
3. Repeat silently to yourself information that you are recording so that you won't forget it before writing it down?
4. Identify possible test questions?
5. Self test by answering questions from memory, or by writing out key concepts from memory?
6. Use a variety of methods to develop a good memory of the content (such as using examples, reorganizing information into tables and diagrams, recitation, and self testing)?
7. Keep track of the stated aims and objectives of the course (e.g., by periodically reading the course outline and listening for messages from the instructor)?
8. Review regularly to reduce forgetting?

Total

Add up the total checkmarks in the yes and no columns. If you have many more yes's than no's then you are on the right track. However, if you are heavily into no's then you need to make some changes.

PUBLISHER'S NOTE TO INSTRUCTORS AND STUDENTS

This text book is a key component of your course. If you are the instructor of this course, you undoubtedly considered a number of texts carefully before choosing this as the one that will work best for your students and you. The authors and publishers of this book spent considerable time and money to ensure its high quality, and we appreciate your recognition of this effort and accomplishment.

If you are a student, we are confident that this text will help you to meet the objectives of your course. You will also find it helpful after the course is finished, as a valuable addition to your personal library. So hold on to it.

As well, please don't forget that photocopying copyright work means the authors lose royalties that are rightfully theirs. This loss will discourage them from writing another edition of this text or other books, because doing so will simply not be worth their time and effort. If this happens, we all lose — students, instructors, authors, and publishers.

And since we want to hear what you think about this book, please be sure to send us the stamped reply card at the end of the text. This will help us to continue publishing high-quality books for your courses.

1. INTRODUCTION TO SUCCESSFUL LEARNING

- Welcome to the book

- The successful learner

- The good strategy user

- You as a good strategy user

- Important general strategies

- Where can I begin?

- An example of a planful strategy — Goal setting

- Your immediate goals?

- Effective strategies and roadblocks

WELCOME TO THE BOOK

When you listen to people talking about a student's progress you will often hear terms such as 'bright', 'average', and 'poor'. As we learn more and more about the learning process, we begin to realize how complex learning is and we do not label the process in such simplistic terms. Learning involves very many factors in addition to natural abilities, such as home background and experiences, personality, formal schooling, and motivation.

One component of successful performance that you control is the set of strategies that you apply to your studies and the resultant learning skills. Learning skills are the skills that, as a student, help you to handle the amount and array of information coming from different sources. They are the skills that you apply to listening, note taking, reading, reviewing, essay/assignment preparation, and the management of study time in order to get the most out of these activities. By developing your learning skills you can increase your satisfaction in the role of student, knowing that you are putting forward the effort that you have determined is right for you.

One of the keys to personal control of your studying is awareness of yourself as a learner, knowing what you do and why you do it, and being on the alert for cues about changes you may need to make. Self-awareness, monitoring, and personal control are recurrent themes throughout this book.

In each of the chapters there are many suggestions on approaches to learning. Some of these suggestions will not be new to you. Students at colleges and universities have already acquired study patterns. Reading about learning strategies and skills will reinforce the usefulness of those you have already. However, it is hoped that there will also be new ideas that you will consider using.

No two students are ever exactly alike in their approach to studying. Successful strategies vary with the individual. Where suggestions are presented in this book they are presented as possible strategies. Select those that you think may be useful for you, but give those which you try time to work for you. Study habits are like any other habits. Once they are established they are difficult to dislodge. It takes a certain amount of effort to discard them if they are ineffective, and then to develop new habits. However, in the long run your newly acquired habits may save you a lot of time and frustration.

THE SUCCESSFUL LEARNER

Melanie is a first-year student who has just got back a test result in her introductory history course. She can't wait to get back to residence to share the great news with her roommate Karen that her very first test mark is an 'A'.

Karen responds just as she expected with a wild yell and dances around the room, but then flops on the bed and looks at her. "You know", she says, "I'm not at all surprised that you got that 'A' because:

1._____

_____

_____

2._____

_____

_____

3._____

_____

_____

How do you think that Karen is explaining Melanie's success? Can you fill in some of the reasons why her mark was an 'A'? Try to list at least three reasons before reading further.

THE GOOD STRATEGY USER

One explanation that modern educators might give for Melanie's 'A' grade is that Melanie is a *good strategy user*[1]. This view contrasts with a more traditional view in education that would say that the main reasons for Melanie's 'A' are that Melanie is bright, that is she has a high I.Q., and that she works hard. While those two factors may be important, there is a lot of evidence to suggest that performance in school is often based on learned strategies that are used appropriately. Success is not just a matter of innate ability and hours and hours of study.

Let us take a closer look at four components that contribute to good strategy use in the case of Melanie:

1. Background General Knowledge

Melanie took History every year in high school, so this introductory course doesn't contain too many surprises. For example, the struggles between the French and the English settlers are not new to her, although never before has she gone into such detailed analysis of the Acadians.

She finds that her previous courses have provided an adequate background, so that she seldom feels overwhelmed or lost in class. In addition, she prepares for each class by reading ahead in the text. She knows that she gets a lot more out of a lecture when she has done her homework thoroughly.

2. Personal Attitudes and Beliefs

Melanie enjoys being a student. Although she does find some things difficult, she believes that she can do well if she both plans her activities and chooses appropriate strategies to meet important goals. She wants a balanced life on campus, and she does not feel guilty taking time out for herself to play squash, knowing that she has planned for that. She is a great believer in both working and playing hard. She is prepared to give things her best shot and right now things are looking good.

---

[1] The term "Good strategy user" was first used in, Pressley, M., J. G. Borkowski, and W. Schneider (1987). "Cognitive strategies: Good strategy users coordinate metacognition and knowledge". *Annals of Child Development*, Vol 4, 89–129. JAI Press Inc.

3. Strategies

Reading the text ahead of class to acquire background knowledge is one specific strategy that works for Melanie. There are many other strategies that she uses in her overall approach, and they all contribute to her good performance. Some of the strategies set up her external learning environment, and others affect how she mentally processes the course content.

EXAMPLES OF ENVIRONMENT SETTING STRATEGIES:

1. She has a favourite quiet corner in the library and she always goes there to read the history text.
2. She sits where the lighting is just right so that her eyes do not get tired.
3. She sets a goal of reading ten pages before taking a short break.

EXAMPLES OF MIND ENGAGING STRATEGIES:

4. As she listens to the lecture she tries to listen for themes and to label them in her notes with headings.
5. She finds time to reread her lecture notes after class, checking to see that she understands her own notes.
6. If there is information that she doesn't understand, she works on that as soon as possible by checking the text, asking another student, or by checking with the instructors.

4. Strategic Awareness (Metacognition)

Strategic awareness (metacognition) refers to what Melanie knows about her own learning, and her ability to control it. So, not only does Melanie have strategies at her disposal, she also knows a lot about when and where to use them. For example, when she has to prepare for a test she may use extra memory devices because she knows that she will need to have more information at her fingertips for the test than she would need going to a regular lecture. She might use a mnemonic in the form of a rhyme or sentence to help her remember some critical facts. Strategies have to be appropriate to the task if they are to be effective.

YOU AS A GOOD STRATEGY USER

How do you rate yourself as a *good strategy user*? Choose one course that you are currently taking and think about the four components of the model:

NAME OF COURSE _____

1. Where did your background knowledge come from for this course and is it adequate for you to keep up with the course without too much difficulty?

_____

_____

2. How do you feel about yourself as a learner? What do you believe about your potential in this course?

_____

_____

_____

3. List any strategies that you consciously use in this course.

_____

_____

_____

4. Give one example of how you have adapted a strategy to meet the special demands of an exam.

_____

_____

_____

IMPORTANT GENERAL STRATEGIES

Although this book introduces very many strategies, it also highlights the following five important general strategies that apply to any subject area, and they provide a theme throughout the book:

1. **Be strategic.** This is the whole message of this book. It encourages students to exercise considerable control over their own learning through their choice of approach to selected tasks. The term "strategy" originated in a military context and encompasses three components, which are: (1) to devise a plan, (2) to reach a goal, (3) in an optimal manner.

   Students often approach tasks in an intuitive manner based largely on past experience of similar situations. However, a strategic approach, with more conscious assessment and planning, is especially important to success in a situation where the task is unfamiliar or difficult for the student. For example, many students report that multiple-choice testing requires very different review strategies to those needed for essay tests.

2. **Be a reflective learner.** This suggests that you try to focus on the way you study. There are many examples of how to do this, but one is to assess periodically how you approach learning. A checklist of strategies is provided at the beginning of this book as an initial invitation to be more reflective. Other inventories will allow you to assess other areas.

3. **Be on the alert for cues.** There are many messages that the academic world gives to students. Some are very direct. For example, an instructor may say, "on the test next week there will be questions only on this term's work", or "in this research essay all of your points must be substantiated with real evidence". These are only two of a possible host of cues that may be given for any course.

   Some of the cues may be more subtle and this problem may arise from the instructor's expectations of the students. He/she may expect that the student already knows basic information necessary to doing well in the course. In fact that assumption may be incorrect. Students who are cue aware are much more likely to work efficiently, appropriately, and to be successful than students who are cue deaf. The main sources of cues are the instructor, the course outline, and other students.

4. **Monitor your progress.** How will you know if you have successfully learned what you intended to learn? You do not want the exam result to be your first feedback on the quality of your learning. In science subjects such as math, physics, and chemistry it is common to solve sets of problems to check the level of your understanding. In many other disciplines though, you have to think of ways to check your own performance. Good students find interesting ways to do this evaluation.

5. **Be a planful learner.** There are many situations in which students need to be planful, such as planning their academic programs to ensure that there will not be major problems of lack of background or work overload. Students need to set the external learning environment by selecting when and where to work, and organizing any resources such as materials and help. Try to be in charge of the things you do by planning ahead. The chapter on time management goes into more detail about planning, but this chapter stresses that for the planful learner it is important to set goals. Goals can be far in the future or relatively immediate. They can be vague or very specific.

WHERE CAN I BEGIN?

If you wish to work at being a better strategy user, then a good place to begin is with the strategies themselves. At this point we could give you a whole list of strategies to try, tied to do's and don't's — a prescription for the perfect student. However, we know that that would not work for many people. Most students tune out or turn off when presented with too many ideas for change.

A much better approach is for you to *identify for yourself a small number of strategies* that you wish to focus on and develop, and that you believe might work for you. Each chapter of this book introduces many strategies that successful students report work for them. It is important to remember that there are individual differences among students and not all strategies work for everyone. You are the decision maker so you choose which strategies to try.

Earlier we said that study habits are like any other habits. They are difficult to change. You may find that you have to *consciously remind yourself of the strategies you wish to try.* It will take time before you use a strategy automatically. Some students may need to go so far as writing the strategy on a 3″ × 5″ card and posting it where they cannot miss it, or devising some other similar system.

AN EXAMPLE OF A PLANFUL STRATEGY — GOAL SETTING

There are many goals that students set for themselves. Any one student might have the following goals, to:

- live a happy life.
- get into medical school and become a heart surgeon.
- maintain a **B** average this year.
- finish this essay before the due date next week.
- read the sociology chapter tonight.
- solve this math problem within 10 minutes.

As the examples show, goals can range all the way from very vague and/or in the future to specifically task related and very immediate. While it is necessary to set both future-oriented and present-oriented goals, it is the more immediate goals that can really make the difference to achievement and performance. There is no point in having heart surgery as your ultimate career goal if you can never achieve the immediate goal of sitting down to study. However, on the other hand if you are very organized and goal oriented on a day-to-day basis, but have absolutely no idea where your life is going, then you could end up in a blind alley. It is best to set a range of goals, both for the future and for the present.

YOUR IMMEDIATE GOALS?

What study tasks do you plan to complete today?

1. _____

2. _____

3. _____

4. _____

5. _____

EFFECTIVE STRATEGIES AND ROADBLOCKS

What things work for you as a student and what things work against you? Think about this in your next class and also in your personal study time, then use this sheet to collect some information.

	Effective Strategies for Learning	Roadblocks to Learning
Class Time	1. 2. 3.	1. 2. 3.
Study Time	1. 2. 3.	1. 2. 3.

2. ORGANIZING YOUR TIME

- A common problem

- Awareness of present experience

- Recording and analysing time spent

- Strategies for balancing study time with other activities

- Putting these strategies to use

- Strategies for planning your study time

- Putting it all together

- Time troubles

A COMMON PROBLEM

Do you ever wonder how the world's great leaders find time to run their countries on only 24 hours each day? Thinking about such people can help to put things in perspective when you find yourself beginning to panic about getting things done. Time management is a fact of life for everyone, great and small, although there are enormous differences among individuals as to how this is accomplished.

For some, time management takes the "default option" in which things happen, and the individual responds to whatever. Others are rigid controllers with definite plans at all times. However, the majority of us locate somewhere between these two extremes, with many wishing for a more consistent ability to manage time. Like many people, students commonly report dissatisfaction with their personal attempts at time management:

> "My friend dropped by last night and I didn't like to tell him that I had work to do."

> "I'm in a couple of clubs, but I find it tough fitting them in with my course load."

> "I takes me hours to do all the required readings for my weekly history tutorial."

> "I work really hard, but I never seem to get everything done that I should."

This chapter begins with having you assess your own experience with time management. Raising awareness is an important step for anyone wishing to take more control of time planning. This chapter then goes on to introduce management strategies aimed at balancing study time with all of the other activities of life. These are followed by more specific strategies for organizing study tasks for courses. The objective of this chapter is not to convert you into a rigid clock watcher, but to suggest ways of planning to get your studying done so that you can get better results and enjoy your leisure time without feeling guilty.

AWARENESS OF PRESENT EXPERIENCE

For each question, check the response that best fits your personal experience. After you have finished the exercise, you may wish to reflect on your overall satisfaction with your current time management experience.

1. Never or rarely   2. Sometimes   3. Often or always

		1	2	3
1.	Have you got a system for planning each day?	——	——	——
2.	Do you feel pressured by others to join in their activities?	——	——	——
3.	Do you have time to do the things you want to do?	——	——	——
4.	Do you really worry about getting things done?	——	——	——
5.	Do you feel in control of your schedule?	——	——	——
6.	Is time management a problem for you?	——	——	——
7.	Do your own friends practise good time management?	——	——	——
8.	Do you find yourself racing from one deadline to another?	——	——	——
9.	Do you have a clear idea of where your time goes?	——	——	——
10.	Are you too busy to eat right or exercise regularly?	——	——	——
11.	Do you talk with friends and instructors about time management problems?	——	——	——
12.	Do things often pile up?	——	——	——
13.	Do you feel satisfied with the way you plan your time?	——	——	——
14.	Do you often give up because things overwhelm you?	——	——	——

RECORDING AND ANALYSING TIME SPENT

If you are having difficulty altering a pattern of time use to suit your needs, try monitoring your time use for three weekdays. Use the following chart to record your activities, hour by hour. Pay particular attention to out-of-class study time. Use the information recorded to find out how much time you are spending on different activities by completing the tables on the next page.

	MONDAY	TUESDAY	WEDNESDAY	THURSDAY	FRIDAY
7:00					
8:00					
9:00					
10:00					
11:00					
12:00					
1:00					
2:00					
3:00					
4:00					
5:00					
6:00					
7:00					
8:00					
9:00					
10:00					
11:00					

ACTIVITIES	HOURS			
	DAY 1	DAY 2	DAY 3	TOTAL
CLASS				
STUDY				
TRAVEL				
EXERCISE				
MEALS & CHORES				
LEISURE				
SLEEP				
TOTAL				

1.   Fill in the total STUDY time for each course. List the tasks that were done.

COURSE	TIME	TASKS
1.		
2.		
3.		
4.		
5.		

2. Can you see which times of day are good for

  • serious concentration?_____

  • demanding study tasks?_____

3. Can you detect a time that is not productive for studying?

_____

_____

STRATEGIES FOR BALANCING STUDY TIME WITH OTHER ACTIVITIES

1. **Plan ahead.** The pace of college and university life is not always the same. At times, studying takes on a particular urgency as you complete a major assignment or study for a crucial test. At other times, extra-curricular activities take high priority. You may be in the playoffs as a member of the hockey team, producing a play or making important decisions on student council. Unfortunately, many students are not used to planning ahead. This becomes particularly evident around the busy times of each semester, especially exam periods. A successful strategy for anticipating the "crunch" times is to mark down deadlines on a calendar posted in a prominent location, or to write them down in a dayplanner. Even spending a few minutes daily or weekly thinking about the combination of activities ahead can make a difference.

2. **Write things down.** When planning ahead, we can usually remember a small number of tasks in our heads. However, this method becomes less and less reliable as the number of tasks increases. When faced with many tasks to do, writing down what must be done can be very helpful. Again, there is a variety of ways to do this: some people swear by detailed weekly schedules whereas others like brief, daily or weekly lists.

3. **Make each day count.** Aim to get some high priority tasks completed each day. Even small, regular accomplishments can make a big hole in the total amount that you have to get done. Some time managers refer to this as the "Swiss Cheese" approach!

4. **Know and use your best times.** There are certain times in each day when one seems to be able to do tasks requiring concentration very efficiently. On the other hand, there are other times of the day when it is more difficult to make progress. For instance, many people find they can study well in the morning whereas before supper it is much harder for them to take in course material. When are your best times for studying? Whenever possible, do you try to use these times for studying or do these best times get spent on other less important activities?

5. **Use small blocks of time.** Many useful hours in the week are wasted by students who think that an hour between classes is not enough time to get anything

accomplished. Much important learning can and should be done in an hour or less: reviewing class notes, reading part of a chapter, doing a few problems, going to see a instructor. Indeed a number of successful students report that this is their most important time management strategy.

6. **Plan for meals and recreation.** Although it is important to look after your academic needs, it is equally important to look after other needs as well. A healthy lifestyle is crucial to enjoyment of student life and to your ability to study effectively. However, this also requires some planning — time for nutritious meals (especially a breakfast with some protein), regular exercise, and a reasonable amount of leisure time for relaxation. Unfortunately. many students get into the vicious circle of short-changing health, and thus efficiency, in a futile effort to get more done.

7. **Establish a regular routine.** Studying can become more automatic if you plan study tasks in the same time slots each week. This reduces the amount of energy required for making day-by-day decisions.

PUTTING THESE STRATEGIES TO USE

On the next page is one student's sample weekly schedule. You can see that this student is using a number of the strategies just discussed. First of all this student has worked out her potential study times for each day that include some blocks of time during the day. She has tried to use her best times for studying, i.e., after supper and in the morning. Furthermore, she has set aside ample time for meals, recreation, and time off every evening after 10:00 p.m. and on the weekends. Interestingly, this schedule allows our student to get more than 25 hours of good learning accomplished each week.

Use the blank schedule on page 19 to plan your potential and flexible study periods, keeping in mind the strategies discussed.

| | POTENTIAL STUDY PERIOD | | | FLEXIBLE STUDY PERIOD |

	Monday	Tuesday	Wednesday	Thursday	Friday	Saturday	Sunday
7:00–8:00	←	—	*Breakfast*	—	→		
8:00–9:00		↑		MATH TUTORIAL	↑ GEOG		
9:00–10:00		Bio LAB	↑		LAB ↓		
10:00–11:00		↓	CHEM LAB				
11:00–12:00	Swim	GEOG. 20	↓	GEOG. 20	Lunch		
12:00–1:00	MATH 23	Lunch	MATH 23	Lunch	MATH 23		
1:00–2:00	Lunch	PHYSICS 20	Lunch	PHYSICS 20			
2:00–3:00	CHEM 20		CHEM 20	↑			
3:00–4:00	Bio ↑		Squash	PHYSICS LAB			
4:00–5:00	20 ↓	Swim	Swim	↓	Swim		
5:00–6:00	←		*Dinner*		→		
6:00–7:00				↑ Squash			
7:00–8:00				Club			
8:00–9:00				↓			
9:00–10:00							
10:00–11:00							

	Monday	Tuesday	Wednesday	Thursday	Friday	Saturday	Sunday
7:00–8:00							
8:00–9:00							
9:00–10:00							
10:00–11:00							
11:00–12:00							
12:00–1:00							
1:00–2:00							
2:00–3:00							
3:00–4:00							
4:00–5:00							
5:00–6:00							
6:00–7:00							
7:00–8:00							
8:00–9:00							
9:00–10:00							
10:00–11:00							

STRATEGIES FOR PLANNING YOUR STUDY TIME

1. **Set priorities.** Priorities need to be set on two levels; first of all among all of your courses, and also among tasks within each course. Certain courses will require more time and energy than others; so, plan your study time to reflect those special needs. Also, certain tasks within a course may have greater payoff in developing competency, and consequently may result in higher marks. It is surprising how often students do not set priorities to reflect the way in which the course is evaluated. For example, a student may spend many hours on a report worth 10 marks and only a few hours of review for a test worth 25 marks.

2. **Beware of courses you like/dislike.** This strategy is directly related to the previous one, and is mentioned specifically because so many students make the error of studying long hours on courses they like and very little on courses they dislike. Because these students have "studied a lot", they are often surprised when they do poorly on courses they disliked.

3. **Plan your study environment.** There are some places where one can get a lot of work accomplished, and others where little or nothing gets done. The ideal study location may vary somewhat from one student to another, but many students report that they prefer locations that are quiet, well lit, free from distractions, and "appropriately" comfortable. You may need to experiment by studying in a variety of locations to find which one works best for you.

4. **Set small, specific study goals.** Often students sit down to study with the idea of doing three straight hours in one subject. Those three hours can look awfully long and boring, so procrastination usually sets in: the room is cleaned, pencils sharpened, friends drop in. A much more effective way of studying is to set small study goals that can be achieved in an hour or less, e.g., "I will read 10 pages of the text in Economics" or "I will do 4 math problems".

5. **Take short breaks regularly.** When a small study goal is achieved, give yourself a short break of 5 to 10 minutes. Have a drink of water or walk around a bit, but don't start something that is difficult to stop such as watching TV or starting a deep discussion unless you have finished studying. Appropriate small breaks in long study sessions can refresh you for further efficient learning.

6. **Brief, same-day review of lecture notes.** This can be a very powerful time-saving strategy. By doing some kind of active but brief review of your lecture notes on or near the day of that lecture you can save many hours of "relearning" (see chapter 5 on Learning from Lectures for more details).

7. **Distribute learning of memory material.** With courses in which there is a lot of detailed information to memorize, e.g., biology, psychology, and economics, it is a good idea to spread the learning over a number of separate study periods. Three one-hour study periods spaced throughout the week are more effective than a single three-hour chunk.

8. **Massed learning for project tasks.** Project tasks, such as essays, case studies, and lab reports, should be tackled in fairly large blocks of time. These activities often require the integration of a variety of sources in order to accomplish deeper levels of insight and organization. Even within such massed learning, it is still useful to set subgoals and take short breaks.

9. **Get started.** You plan to spend the evening working at home, but before you begin you make a cup of coffee ... clear off your desk top ... change into a track suit ... flick through a magazine and ... if any of these activities sound familiar then you need to think through some strategies that will combat this form of procrastination.

PUTTING IT ALL TOGETHER

You have read through the many general strategies for managing time as a whole, and also those strategies specific to planning study tasks. Now you need to find some consistent way of putting strategies together so that the whole process of managing time is planned effectively. Although the following suggestions are quite specific, they are to be used only as a guide. You need to work at finding the system that is best suited to your own personal learning style.

STEP	GOAL	STRATEGIES
1	MOTIVATION	1. Decide that you wish to take control of your own time planning.
2	ASSESSMENT	1. List all of the activities that you need to, or would like to, find time for. 2. Estimate how much time per week each activity will require. 3. Consider whether each activity will occur regularly or occasionally.
3	PRIORITIES	1. Label each activity as either essential or optional. 2. Rank each on a scale of high/medium /low priority.
4	PLANNING	1. Mark important assignment and test dates on a yearly calendar. 2. Post a timetable with all regular class times indicated. 3. Use a diary, or other preferred system, to plan a tentative schedule of study tasks you wish to accomplish in a week. You may not follow it rigidly, but it will guide your daily planning. Keep in mind a) best times to study, and b) using small time blocks.

		4. Each evening plan carefully, and *write down*, your goals for the following day. 5. Collect together all necessary notes and texts for the following day.
5	ENVIRONMENT	1. Find a quiet, comfortable place to study. 2. Make sure that you have all the necessary materials. 3. Check your goals for the day. 4. Set a small study goal for what you wish to accomplish in the next short period (20–50 minutes).
6	STUDY	1. Get started. 2. Work to achieve each small study goal you have set. 3. Take short appropriate breaks to keep your energy and concentration levels high. 4. Check off the tasks on your daily plan as you complete them.
7	EVALUATION	1. Reschedule tasks that need additional time to complete. 2. Ask yourself the question, "Do I feel good about what I achieved today?" 3. Decide if your tentative schedule for the remainder of the week needs reviewing. 4. If you are still experiencing real time management problems, you should probably discuss the issue with a friend, instructor or counsellor.

TIME TROUBLES

1. Andrew has been spending more and more of his time talking with his friends rather than preparing for his classes. He's frequently so involved he forgets to go to lectures. He often says he has problems controlling his time. *What suggestions do you have for working on his problem?*

2. Maria, a first-year student, is carrying six subjects. She feels a great amount of pressure because her family has sacrificed for her education. She's having difficulty managing her time plus she's been offered a part-time job. *What comments would you make on her situation?*

3. Michele has come to university to meet new people and expand her horizons. Her studies are important to her, but she also wants to have an active social life. This is the second week of class and she hasn't done any studying so far. *If you were to meet her, what advice and help would you offer?*

4. Daniel would like to be on student council. He also wants to get into medical school and is in a demanding first-year science programme. *How can he accommodate these two goals?*

3. PROCRASTINATION AND OTHER TIME TROUBLES

- The stress of studying

- Reasons for procrastination

- The vicious circle

- Worry thoughts

- Remedies for procrastination

- Concentration

- Your concentration profile

THE STRESS OF STUDYING

Planning realistically for upcoming assignments and tests usually leads to success. However, some students report that they cannot follow-up on their good intentions, even with a plan. Others again confess to giving up on planning completely and just trying to keep up with one deadline after another. They are experiencing some of the stress of being students who are in doubt about their chances of success. Here are a few typical comments:

"I really didn't choose my elective very well — I just don't think I have enough background to understand it."

"I never feel caught-up in this course — it moves along so quickly."

"I'm never sure how I'll do in multiple-choice tests — even after I've finished them."

"I didn't do anything this week. There were so many things to do that I didn't dare begin."

"I'm not even sure that I want to be here. It's not the fun place that I expected. I do nothing but work, work, work."

These students are responding to the change in expectations and workload of moving to a post-secondary setting. Though many enjoy this change as stimulating, for some students who have relied on guidance about what to do and how they are doing, these new challenges seem unnerving. Students in this group often report that they find themselves procrastinating on course assignments and being frustrated at not getting things accomplished. These problems can lead to more worry and also to common concentration problems.

REASONS FOR PROCRASTINATION

When we asked a group of students about their reasons for procrastinating, they came up with several suggestions:

1. **Inertia.** This prevents some people being able to change from one activity to another. It takes less energy to keep on doing the same thing — especially if it is having a cup of coffee or watching T.V.

2. **Loose ends.** Some people feel it is important to finish one thing completely before going on to another.

3. **So much work.** With many things to do — all claiming equal priority — it is hard to decide where to begin, and so it is easier not to.

4. **Low appeal.** Other activities seem to have more pay-off than studying, especially in the short term, e.g., sports, socializing, going to the movies.

5. **Loneliness.** Studying is isolating. So many tasks have to be done alone.

6. **Guilt.** What is being neglected for study? Other things require your time and attention, e.g., your friends, family, church, ... the dog.

7. **Fear of failure.** Last time you tried to read this chapter it didn't go very well ... and you can remember not being able to get these math problems ... now you are confused about what to expect.

8. **Fear of success.** What will happen if you do well? Your expectations will go up. Other people might have them too ... you might not get so much help ...

THE VICIOUS CIRCLE

Just as students are experts at analysing the reasons for procrastination, they can be adept at finding alternative activities that seem to be worthwhile. Spending time at the gym (it's good to be fit), organizing a club (great experience for my résumé) or volunteering to help at the hospital (valuable career exploration) can all be substitutes for studying.

When this is happening, most students are aware of their procrastination, but they cannot seem to break out of a vicious circle of messages that are self-critical and discouraging. Considerable worry may result from attempts to control this problem.

Many of us have valid doubts about how well we are performing, but in the vicious circle these become so overwhelming that they prevent us from getting down to studying and result in poor concentration. Then the distractions of social and recreational opportunities offer temporary relief by "putting things off". Even while avoiding the issue, however, we are still feeling guilty about what is being neglected.

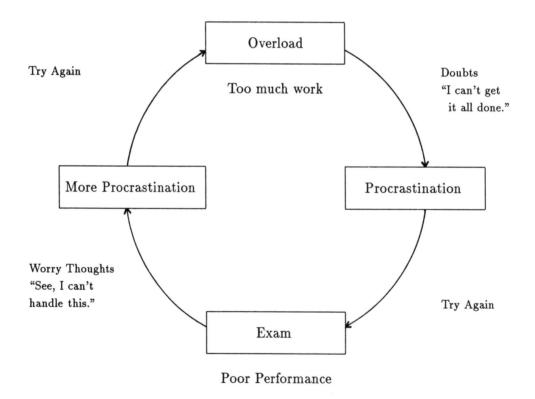

WORRY THOUGHTS

Worry thoughts can not only be very distracting but, more significantly, can lead to physical symptoms of stress. Tension headaches, sleeplessness, and stomach upsets are a few such symptoms. Once there is such a physical response, it can be much more difficult to rewrite that "internal script". A spontaneous reaction is to take time out and rest, but this is, at best, only a temporary solution. The basic issue of how to put positive energy into studying will still remain.

It is, therefore, important to be able to monitor both your symptoms of stress and the kind of worry thoughts to which you attend. If you see study tasks as threats to which you respond with fear or anxiety, you will have a different physical response to that of a student who perceives the situation as a challenge that can be a trigger for excitement rather than fear. You may have to write down some of your worry thoughts in order to assess what assumptions you are making about your approach to studying.

One exercise that can be useful is to compare your mental messages about studying with your thoughts about something you really enjoy, such as playing a game of tennis. The chances are that when enjoying the activity, you do not find mistakes such a problem, you can keep your mind on the here and now, and you are not too concerned with the results. On the other hand, students under stress about study tasks become upset about mistakes, spend time wondering about what will happen *if* they don't do well, and dwell on a negative outcome, such as low marks.

Because such negative thoughts do seem to have an effect on behaviour, it is often helpful to rehearse statements that are more positive and may keep your attention in the present, e.g., "What's involved here?" or "What's the next step?" Getting help from a counsellor in order to monitor your thought process could be very valuable, for this has been found to be a way of improving your ability to cope with the stress of study. More about anxiety is explained in Chapter 11: WRITING EXAMS, p. 121.

There are certainly times when all of us become caught in the vicious circle and have to consciously work to keep moving. With this in mind, the following ideas, gleaned from students, may provide a useful starting point.

REMEDIES FOR PROCRASTINATION

1. Set up a reward for finishing something; this can counteract a lack of initiative.
2. Select a task to start with that is not too demanding — in your estimation.
3. Subdivide a bigger task into several chunks (e.g., 15-minute items); this can reduce difficulty.
4. Suspend your criticism of how well you are doing in order to get through it at least once.
5. Co-operate with a friend in sharing an assignment by working in tandem; this can reduce the isolation.
6. Substitute the mental message "I should" with "I'd like to".
7. Lower your expectations and accept that a realistic goal is "doing your best within a time limit".
8. Assess how you might improve your concentration.

CONCENTRATION

Concentration is being able to direct one's attention or giving all one's attention to one thing. How can some students sit down and concentrate fully, whereas others find themselves daydreaming or attending to various diffuse thoughts or disturbances around them?

Achieving better concentration is very important to making your study time most effective. Two or three hours of intense effort are worth a day of interrupted or haphazard study.

This chapter will present three important components of concentration, and suggest strategies that you can adopt that will help to bring your attention to focus more readily on one task. These are:

Commitment
Knowing why (or convincing yourself that) the study task at hand is important.

Internal Distractions
Using strategies to deal with wandering thoughts.

External Distractions
Organizing a place and time for studying that helps you to shut out things going on around you.

Commitment

Your level of concentration while studying is closely linked to your interest in the subject matter of a course, the way in which it is taught, the setting, and whether or not it is an optional or mandatory course choice. Strategies that can help to maintain a high level of commitment to a course are:

1. *Find out as much as you can about a course before choosing to take it.* Read the calendar description, talk to the instructor, and talk to students who have taken the course, if possible. Check that your background is adequate for you to handle the course without major problems, and that you feel confident about the work load.

2. *Assess the contribution that the course will make to your general knowledge base, your degree program, and to possible career choices.* Your commitment will be stronger if you have a clear idea of the benefits of the course.

3. *Know the rules and regulations governing the course.* If you have a clear idea of whether or not you can withdraw from a course if things go poorly, you will not feel so trapped about giving it reasonable effort.

4. *If you anticipate any problems, you may wish to be part of a study group.* In difficult courses, it is not uncommon for students to share ideas about them.

5. *Try to work regularly at the course.* It is difficult to maintain a high level of commitment when you fall behind and get overwhelmed by the amount of work ahead of you.

Can you identify your commitment to the courses you are currently taking? For each course, try to give at least one reason for your choice.

	COURSE	REASON FOR TAKING COURSE
1.		
2.		
3.		
4.		
5.		

Internal Distractions

You can be distracted from studying if you are physically uncomfortable. You may be too cold or too hot, hungry or too full. The light level may be straining your eyes, or the position in which you are studying may become uncomfortable. Try to organize these things at the beginning of the study period. Your determination to pursue your studying in an active way can be gauged by whether or not you can use some of the following strategies to aid concentration:

1. *Record a pencil checkmark when your mind wanders from the topic at hand.* Monitoring the number of check marks will give you a way of checking if your attention span is improving.

2. *Try "thought stopping" when you find yourself daydreaming.* Some reflection — especially if some personal emergencies are interfering — can be productive; but if this happens too often, say "Stop" mentally and then redirect your attention back to the work you are doing.

3. *Define a specific objective for a fairly short time span.* This can avoid the vagueness of an approach such as "I'll do as much as I can on Tuesday evening." Saying "I'm going to read 5 pages of sociology and make up three questions on them" can give you a realistic goal to work toward.

4. *Set up a method of self-testing on the work you have covered in any hour.* Knowing that you have to complete this will keep your focus on the task. Using it will increase your ability to recall material.

5. *Use a problem-solving technique to deal with a persistently disturbing thought*, e.g., "Should I work part-time or not?"

    a) Move away from where you are studying.
    b) Decide what is the concern.
    c) Look at why it is difficult to make the choice.
    d) List the pros and cons of the possible solutions.
    e) Consider whether you can decide on your own or if you need to consult with others.
    f) Plan when and how you will deal with it.
    g) Note this down and return to your studying.

External Distractions

Although finding a time and place for studying with few distractions will not guarantee concentration, it will make it easier for you to control your attention. Most of us can attend to only one main train of thought at a time. In your study experience, how difficult to ignore are these following distractions?

		Easy to Ignore	More Difficult to Ignore	Impossible to Ignore
1.	Hearing a conversation near your desk.			
2.	Sensing doors opening and shutting.			
3.	Hearing the radio or T.V. in the same room.			
4.	Noticing traffic outside the room.			
5.	Hearing specific loud noises, e.g., bells, sirens.			
6.	Being interrupted by someone.			

Students will give different answers to this list though few can ignore the last item. Students who regularly work well in a particular setting learn to expect to concentrate in that place. This may also hold true for working at certain times of the day. Maintaining concentration will be easier if you:

a) Clear your desk of souvenirs, pictures, etc. so that you cannot be distracted by them.

b) Arrange your desk to face a blank wall — your studying must be more interesting than that!

c) Know which libraries suit you — experiment until you find one in which you like to study.

d) Have the right level of noise in the background. Some students claim that they work better with a level of "white noise"; others like silence. Try different situations.

YOUR CONCENTRATION PROFILE

1. Assume that you want to give your full concentration to a task. In the space below describe the ideal situation that will allow you complete concentration.

_____

_____

_____

_____

_____

_____

2. We all have problems sometime or another with concentrating on a task. Imagine you are reading a chapter in a chemistry or sociology text. After 20 minutes, you feel like giving up because you realize that you are not getting anything out of it. List some possible reasons for this.

_____

_____

_____

_____

_____

_____

4. EFFECTIVE MEMORY

- The learning process

- Memory systems

- What works for you?

- Selection frameworks

- A systems exercise

THE LEARNING PROCESS

The aim of this chapter is to highlight some current theories and ideas about the learning process and, in particular, memory systems, so that you can understand better why learning strategies work or do not work in a variety of settings for different individuals.

As you read, keep in mind that *it is you that you are reading about*. The theory will only be of use to you if you can personalize it to your own situation. Keep asking the following questions: "How does the theory reflect my own way of studying?" and "What changes do I need to make as a result of reading this?"

Also, remember that this is theory and that you can question whether or not it seems to fit with your own experience. Learning after all is covert, an internal operation. Any one learner is intimately aware only of her/his own experience. However, current educational theories can contribute much to our knowledge and understanding of ourselves as learners.

Learning-process research focusses on the way in which learning takes place, rather than simply on the products of learning. The products are much more visible and easier to evaluate. They are the test performance, the essay, the solved science problem. In fact, they are the sum total of the knowledge that a student is able to display for others. Here though our interest is on the processes that lead to those end products.

It is important to note that mental processes sometimes occur automatically and sometimes consciously. Many components of behaviour, when doing common tasks such as driving a car or kicking a soccer ball, become automatic through constant use. It is also true that we automatically mentally respond to many learning situations. It is likely that a number of your study habits require little conscious thought, and consequently may be difficult to change. As you read about the learning process, think about how you can have more control of that process through strategies that you consciously choose to apply.

MEMORY SYSTEMS

Educators distinguish three memory systems operating together but with distinct functions and characteristics. They are described very briefly here, focussing on the major implications for a learner who wishes to have more personal control over the learning process. They are:

1. Sensory memory

2. Short-term memory

3. Long-term memory

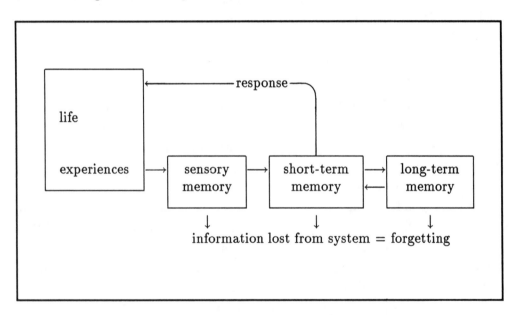

Fig. 4.1   A Theoretical View of Memory

1. Sensory Memory

Our senses, such as sight, hearing, touch, smell, register information from the environment and make it available for further processing in short-term memory. An important feature of the sensory memory system is that information registers only for a very brief period of time. It is then either lost from the system as forgetting or is a conscious thought in short-term memory.

How is this significant for the learner? Well, one might view sensory memory as a critical gateway through which information must pass in order to be available to further memory systems. If information cannot get into and through sensory memory, then it is unavailable to the learner. For information to pass to short-term memory, the learner must give it attention by concentrating on it.

We do not register everything. For example, when we sit at a desk we do not usually notice the pressure of our feet on the floor, or hear constant noise such as a fan, or traffic outside. If we did register everything from our immediate environment, life would be very confusing. A good student has the ability to focus on critical stimuli. Much of what sensory memory registers is either information that has tremendous impact, or that is tied to goals that we set. Your learning goals have a profound effect on the information that you attend to.

2. Short-Term Memory

This is a very active, immediate memory system. It is sometimes referred to as working memory because it is here that a student works to understand and respond to incoming stimuli, whether they come from the external environment or from knowledge retrieved from long-term storage.

Two characteristics of short-term memory are critical to the learner. The first is that information is soon lost from this memory unless it is rehearsed. Most will identify with having to repeat a telephone number if there is a pause between looking up that number and then dialing it. An academic example is of being in a lecture and having to cope with the simultaneous activities of listening to new information while recording previous thoughts. Unless some internal dialogue occurs that allows for repetition of a critical thought, then that information may be forgotten and unavailable for the record.

Also, short-term memory has limited capacity. Although several ideas can be juggled at once, the addition of too many new ideas can result in the loss of some of them. Students need to be very aware of situations that can lead to overload. A good example is when a student reads many pages of text without employing conscious strategies leading to long-term storage of the information. As each new sentence is processed, the load on short-term memory increases and soon the student is in a situation where as much forgetting is taking place as learning.

3. Long-Term Memory

Perfect long-term memory is the dream of many students — who often have tales to tell about all the people they know with fantastic memories. There are the roommates who never study and yet go into tests and always get **A**s. Although it is certainly true that some people appear to be able to remember without much effort, it is also true that many many people, including very good students, have to employ conscious strategies for remembering important information.

How do good students remember key information? We can gain some insight into this problem from research findings and from self-reports from successful learners themselves. Many of these findings can be summarized through the following four important general strategies for effective knowledge storage and retrieval:

1. Select (reduce)
2. Organize
3. Associate
4. Rehearse (review)

1. *SELECT* (Reduce)

Many students report using strategies to reduce the total amount of information to its key elements or main ideas. For a physics student, this might involve distinguishing between general formulae and those applicable only in specific instances, and then working through selected problems. A sociology student might generate a glossary of terms and organize them under main approaches within the discipline. A business student might list a logical sequence of steps in the decision-making process within a company. In other words, the task of reducing information must be appropriate to both the subject matter and to the student's goals for the information. (See pages 42–48 for a discussion of selection frameworks.)

2. *ORGANIZE*

Can you imagine a government office without a filing system? As each new memo and document comes in, it is tossed on a pile in the corner. You can picture the chaos when anyone needs to retrieve an important item! Thankfully, this is not an analogy of the brain. There is a lot of evidence to suggest that information is stored in the form of schema, or organized categories, similar to a sophisticated filing system.

For example, when you read the word 'canary', what are some of the immediate images that you have? In what kind of schema is your canary? Some students report — all things yellow — or birds — or pets. Schema vary considerably among individual students, and there is no question that the personal system that you have developed affects your retrieval abilities. Some personal systems are better than others, and you will wish to work on producing a good system.

Thus, an important goal for a student is to organize information that is to be learned. The probability of information being remembered will be much higher if it is logically organized into units labelled with headings, and using numbers, tables, and diagrams, and also indicating relationships with symbols, arrows, etc.

3. ASSOCIATE

Very closely allied with organization is the way in which new knowledge is associated with existing knowledge. New knowledge is like a ship that needs anchoring in harbour so that it will stay in place. The more associations you make between old and new, the better anchored the new information will be.

Some associations will be *real associations* from your own experience. In sociology, for example, an institution such as the family will be measured against your real family, and visual images of family members, relationships, and events will play a key role in your memory of the concepts.

Not all new information can be matched with real experience, however, and you may need to make *arbitrary associations* to memorize information. An example is the use of mnemonics (memory devices). Words or phrases or visual imagery can be used in this way. *Sohcahtoa* is one word capturing some important trigonometrical principles: sine is opposite over hypotenuse; cosine is adjacent over and so on. Most students have had experience with mnemonics, even if only for remembering the number of days in a month.

4. REHEARSE (Review)

Rehearsal is a powerful form of review. It involves using knowledge in the same way that you will be expected to use it in key situations such as test taking. For example, if you have to write essays for a history test, then it is necessary to write as you learn the information. In such a situation, many students make the mistake of reading and reading. When it comes to the exam, they find themselves having to recall and write for the first time. By self-testing, through writing from memory, you get important feedback on what you do and do not know, as well as practice in communication skills.

In multiple choice exams, there is heavy emphasis on concepts clearly defined. If possible, practise on sample test questions from old tests or from a study guide, if one is available. If sample questions are unavailable, generate short-answer questions and answer them the following day. It is really important to devise ways to use and test information. You do not want the test to be the first time that you have had to recall information from memory.

In problem-solving courses, such as math and physics, much more learning takes place from actively solving problems than from simply reading through concepts.

WHAT WORKS FOR YOU?

Do you know how you memorize information? Think about one of your courses and try to recall some of the key ideas. Try to explain your strategies for remembering.

Course: _____

Strategies for remembering information:

1. _____

_____

2. _____

_____

3. _____

_____

4. _____

_____

SELECTION FRAMEWORKS

Often students find they are bombarded with an immense amount of information in a university course, from which they need to select key points. Somehow, through experience and a good dose of "intuition", many students manage to do this successfully. Others, however, find themselves confused and overwhelmed. One very effective strategy is for students to develop and to use "selection framework" to guide the identification of key ideas from lectures or textbooks. The two selection frameworks introduced here highlight alternative ways to structure knowledge. It must be emphasized that they are not mutually exclusive, and also that they are not carved in stone. That is, students can develop selection frameworks specific to a given course.

An Argument-Based Selection Framework

In this model, emphasis is on the evaluation of phenomena. For any concept, hypotheses are generated, evidence gathered, criticisms evaluated, and general theories proposed. This framework is commonly used in history, political science, psychology, and many other subjects. A similar framework for use in problem-solving courses is presented in Chapter 7: SCIENCE PROBLEM SOLVING, p. 80.

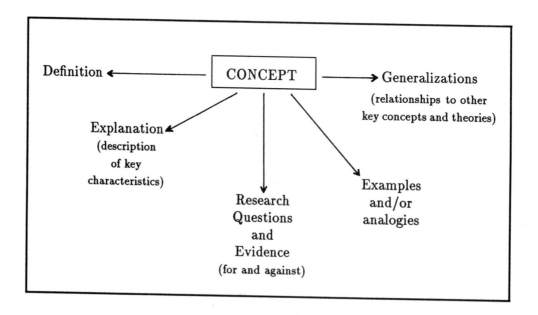

Fig 4.2 An Argument-based selection framework

1. Concept

Concepts are the building blocks of any discipline. However, many students find this term very vague and have difficulty knowing what it means. How can a student recognize the concepts or "key ideas"? There are some strategies to aid this task. If you look through the *course outline*, or any *table of contents* in a textbook, you will immediately focus on some of the major concepts. Also, *titles* and *sub-headings* and *italicized text* usually reflect these major topic areas.

2. Definition

Definitions are not always easily generated even for very familiar concepts; so, it is not uncommon for instructors and writers to define key ideas in several different ways. A common method is to give a functional or working definition, e.g., a tree is a living plant that manufactures food through photosynthesis. An alternative definition might be descriptive, e.g., a tree is a woody plant with roots, a trunk, branches, and leaves.

3. Explanation (description of key characteristics)

Some concepts require more than a simple definition. An explanation of the "what, how or why" of a concept is commonly presented in order to clarify that concept.

4. Research Questions and Evidence (for and against)

This is the crux of the argument-based selection framework. In seeking answers to controversial questions, researchers and scholars present *evidence* in support of their hypotheses or statements. Others may present *criticisms* and refute the arguments. Academic debate is the key component in knowledge growth and change in a discipline.

5. Examples and/or Analogies

The most common technique for clarifying and reinforcing ideas is to use examples and/or analogies. It has already been noted that it is critical for the student to focus on the concept that is being illustrated by the example and/or analogy. It is also important to remember that both examples and analogies are limited in how well they can explain complex ideas.

6. Generalizations (relationships to other key concepts and theories)

The end products of debate are the *conclusions* or *generalizations* made by researchers. Ask yourself the questions, "So what did they find, and what does it all mean?" A natural extension at this point is to explore these meanings in terms of other related concepts and existing theories.

An example from psychology

1. *Concept:* "Positive reinforcer"

2. *Definition:* A reward given for a proper response

3. *Explanation:* Positive reinforcement is associated with instrumental conditioning, a major explanation of learning. Desired behaviour is consistently rewarded, and consequently the behaviour is encouraged.

4. *Research Questions:* Does instrumental learning, as proposed by E. L. Thorndike and further developed by B. F. Skinner, provide a valid explanation of learning?

   (a) *Evidence*

   The behaviourist researchers have conducted many experiments, often using rats or pigeons in controlled situations. A pigeon, in a box, is rewarded with grain after pecking at a lighted key. Initially, the pigeon learns by accident that pecking the key is rewarded with food. As learning proceeds, the pigeon recognizes the lighted key as the stimulus and there is an increase in the rate at which pecking occurs. This evidence supports the concept of a positive reinforcer in instrumental learning.

   (b) *Criticisms*

   Major criticisms have come from cognitive psychologists, who point out that instrumental learning ignores the power of cognitive processes over behaviour in both humans and animals. For instance, monkeys were observed solving problems by insight and with no obvious material reward.

5. *Examples:* A gold star is given to a kindergarten pupil for completing a piece of work. The gold star is assumed to encourage similar desired behaviour in the future.

6. *Generalizations:* By receiving rewards for good behaviour, individuals learn to repeat that same behaviour. This phenomenon of positive reinforcement is applied in many varied contexts: instructors use this concept in classroom management; parents encourage children with rewards; animal trainers depend on the reward system to encourage reliable performance.

A Systems-Based Framework

In some disciplines, the phenomena studied are very complex, and have to be simplified in order to explain and to explore them more easily. One approach to simplification is to use a "general systems" analysis framework. This is common in natural and social sciences such as biology and geography, in engineering, nursing, and many other disciplines. Although the specifics vary with the discipline, they also share much in common, especially the terminology for the components of the system.

1. INPUT. Everything entering the system — can be energy, materials or information.

2. OUTPUT. Everything leaving the system — can be energy, materials or information.

3. SUPRA-SYSTEM. Everything outside the system under study.

4. ORDER OF MAGNITUDE. Systems are hierarchically arranged within broader systems. The level of investigation is arbitrarily set depending on what is studied.

5. STRUCTURAL COMPOSITION. The combination of elements that comprise the system.

6. FUNCTION. The purpose of the system.

7. OPERATING MECHANISMS. Those parts/processes of the system that perform its function.

8. CONSTRAINTS. Anything that may impose limits on, or difficulties for, the system.

9. FLOWS. The transfer of energy, materials or information within the system.

10. FEEDBACK. Flows that circulate within the system. Positive feedback tends to increase the system. Negative feedback tends to decrease the system.

11. CONTROLS. Those parts of the system responsible for its stability or otherwise.

12. HOMEOSTASIS. A steady state — neither expanding or contracting.

A Systems Framework in Biology

Figure 4.3 is a student's schematic representation of terminology generally used in biology courses. Not all terms will be used for each system studied, as illustrated in the student's notes on page 47 for a "closed" circulatory system in animals — the blood.

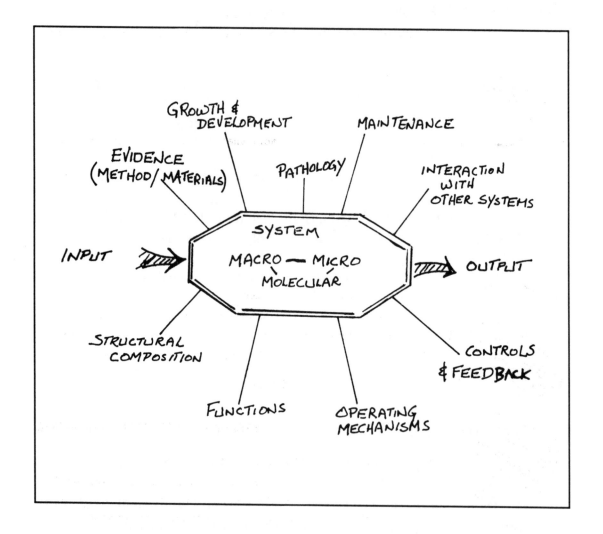

Fig 4.3   Selection Framework for Biological Systems

I. BLOOD: (in circulatory systems of animals)

    A. Functions:

        1. Transport system: gases, nutrients, hormones, etc.

        2. Supplies tissue fluid thru capillary walls to bathe all cells

        3. Coagulates to stop loss from injury

        4. Hydraulic transfer of force, e.g., locomotion of earthworms

    B. Composition: (in general)

        1. Variety of free cells

        2. In liquid plasma

        3. Usually respiratory pigment that colours blood and helps O_2 transport

           e.g., 1. Hemoglobin: red protein, has iron, in cell all vertebr., and some invertebr.

           e.g., 2. Hemocyanin: bluish protein, has copper, dissolved in plasma $\rightarrow$ some invertebr.

    C. Blood (in Vertebrates:)

        1. Erythrocytes: red blood cells

          i) $\approx$ 45% volume of normal blood NB. Hematocrit value

          ii) All vertebr (exc. mammals) Biconvex ovoids w/nucleus

          iii) Mammals (exc. camel) Biconcave ovoid no nucleus

        2. Leucocyte: white blood cells

          i) $\approx$ 1 in 600 cells

          ii) defend organism by phagocytosing foreigners or producing antibodies

          iii) Antibodies: proteins called globulins

             • formed to get invaders or antigens (Immune response)

             • react only to specific antigen by ''recognizing'' sequence of amino acids at molecular binding sites

             • Primary Immune Response: flood of antibodies formed on first exposure to an antigen

             • Secondary Immune Response: leucocytes that formed antibody persist, if antigen returns: lots of antibody produced (faster & better than primary response)

Handwritten margin labels: Functions; Composition; Order of Mag. – Subsystem; Structural Composition; function & mechanism; Control & flows

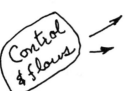

A SYSTEMS EXERCISE

The diagram below is a good example of the use of a general systems framework to describe a very complex real-world phenomenon — commercial agriculture[1]. Because this diagram is so generalized, it could be used in many different contexts simply by changing the subscripts for the elements. For example, it could be used to describe the operating system of a company.

Look at the components of this system and think how they might read if instead this were a model of a major trucking company.

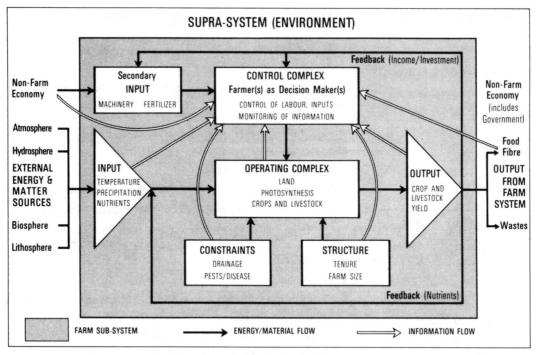

Generalized Control System Relationships for Commercial Agriculture.

Fig 4.5 A Geographic Systems Diagram

---

[1] With permission of the author, Dr. Michael J. Troughton, Department of Geography, The University of Western Ontario.

5. LEARNING FROM LECTURES

- Inventory

- Reading the lecture

- Suggestions for the 'problem' lecture

- Examples of note-taking

- How useful are lecture notes?

INVENTORY

Consider the statements. If possible, answer YES or NO. Fill in any other personal comments about the lecture situation in the blanks.

_____ 1. I usually take notes, but not with much care.

_____ 2. I write down as much as possible of the content of any lecture I attend.

_____ 3. I seldom reread my notes after the lecture.

_____ 4. My notes are never as clear as I would like.

_____ 5. Some lecturers are impossible to follow well enough to take good notes.

_____ 6. My notes are not consistent.

_____ 7. I am not always sure why I write down the things that I do write down.

_____ 8. Taking notes often interferes with my ability to listen carefully.

_____ 9. I always sit in the lecture room where I can see and hear easily.

_____10. If I concentrate on the main ideas, I miss other important facts or details.

_____11. If I find the lecture or lecturer boring, I daydream and don't take down any notes.

_____12. _____

_____13. _____

_____14. _____

_____15. _____

READING THE LECTURE

University or college lectures provide an opportunity for instructor and student to meet and exchange knowledge. Usually, the instructor talks and uses visual aids to present information and ideas, whereas the student listens and records what appear to be the most important points. Both roles are equally important in the exchange because the instructor has to structure the pace and level of information, whereas the student is responsible for listening, questioning, and comprehending the lecture material.

Not all lectures are the same, for they vary according to the discipline, the teaching style, and the student need. In the first few lectures of any course, the instructor and student are becoming acquainted with each other's point of view. Some instructors invite questions and discussion; others prefer to use the lecture to present content and to handle inquiries outside the classroom. Some lectures are highly structured; others are more loosely organized. The student must assess, not only the content of a lecture, but the process in which he/she is participating.

Information about the course is usually supplied by the course outline, which contains information about topics, text, assignments, and evaluation. Each student has to make decisions about which strategies may be most effective in any course. To do this, it is useful to consider the best approach to

1) Listening

2) Recording

3) Editing notes

Pay particular attention to your attitude about lectures. Many students enter the lecture hall with a "ho-hum" mindset, rather than with a keen interest in learning as much as possible.

As you read through this chapter, put a checkmark by any strategy that you do not presently use. When you have finished the chapter, make a decision on which new strategies you will try.

1. Listening

Active listening will help you to get as much as possible from a lecture. You may want to try the following to aid you in lectures.

BEFORE THE LECTURE BEGINS

   a) Survey or read ahead in the text before class in order to recognize new ideas and vocabulary.

   b) Go to class intending to listen. Recognize the active role that you play in the lecture.

   c) Select a place to sit in the classroom where you can keep your attention on the lecturer, and see and hear as well as possible.

   d) Quickly review your notes from the previous class. This will help you to make connections with the previous lecture.

   e) Check the course outline regularly to keep track of the sequence of topics.

DURING THE LECTURE

   a) Listen for opening statements outlining topics, format or philosophy.

   b) Watch the lecturer, not the rest of the class. Spend some time really watching the ways in which the lecturer emphasizes major points through voice, movements, pauses, etc. These cues will help you to discriminate between main ideas and supporting information.

   c) Look out for the way in which the lecturer has organized the material. If it is not well structured, try to organize it for yourself.

   d) Be aware of your general knowledge of the topic. Try to associate it with this new information to give it more meaning.

   e) If you do not understand a point, ask for clarification (either during the lecture or after class).

   f) Be aware of times when your attention may lapse, particularly around the halfway point of the lecture.

Margin notes:

Aids to Listening:

Before Lecture

a. Survey or read ahead

b. Intend to Listen

c. Location

d. Review previous notes

e. Check course outline

During Lecture

a. Opening statements

b. Lecturer's cues

c. Organization of material

d. Your own gen'l knowl.

e. Ask!

f. Attention lapses

What to select?

· *Main ideas*

· *Use abbrev. & incompl. sentences*

· *Use selection framework!*

Strategies

a. *Be early → catch outline*

b. *Writes down.*

c. *Emphasis & Repetition.*

Why Organize Layout?

1. *Learn More*

2. *Easier to read & use*

Strategies

a. *Headings, dates, page #'s.*

2. Recording

SELECTING

As it is not usually possible to write down everything, it is necessary to pick out main ideas while the lecturer is speaking and to make notes. You will find that you need to use abbreviations and incomplete sentences at times to be an efficient note-taker. You will not need to write down everything that is said: only the key information. Use a selection framework as described in Chapter 4: EFFECTIVE MEMORY, p. 35.

Strategies to aid selection:

a) Get to class early to take down any outline that the lecturer may put on the blackboard or overhead.

b) Pay particular attention to the notes that the lecturer writes down in class.

c) Watch for the lecturer's use of emphasis and repetition.

ORGANIZING LAYOUT

You can improve your learning efficiency if you focus on making your notes as organized and as meaningful as possible when you are actually in the lecture. This focus on organization and meaning in the lecture has two benefits: 1) you will learn far more in the lecture itself and thus have much less to do on your own, and 2) your notes will be much easier to read, edit, and review after class.

OVERALL ORGANIZATION OF NOTES

a) Use clear lecture title headings and dates or numbers on each page.

b. One side only

b) Write on only one side of the paper. You can then use the other side of the page to add information from the text, additional examples or review questions.

c. Margin for keynotes

c) Leave a 2" to 3" margin on your note-taking paper, using it to keynote main ideas when you edit notes after class.

d. Loose leaf binder

d) Store lecture notes in loose-leaf binders (as opposed to copybooks) so that you can add handouts, etc.

Ways to Organize Info

WAYS TO ORGANIZE MATERIAL IN NOTES

a. White space

a) Leave lots of white space so that you can add comments later. Also, the notes look better.

b. Set out headings & subheads

b) Select and set out headings and subheadings throughout the material by underlining, indenting, circling, etc.; also likely headings and subheadings. Otherwise, the notes look like paragraphs of prose where little stands out.

c. List with bullets #'s or letters.

c) Under headings and subheadings, list important details with "bullets" or numbers or letters.

d. Graphs & Diagrams: BIG & LABEL!

d) Make graphs and diagrams *big* and *label* them well so that they will be meaningful to you later on.

e. Alternate note structures for diff. kinds of material

e) Decide on alternate note-taking structures for different kinds of material. For example, when ideas are compared you can draw a line down the middle and collect the relevant details on each side. Another example would be branching "flowcharts" for step-by-step decision making.

3. Editing Notes

Research indicates that individuals forget 60% of random information that they hear within 24 hours. If you do not reread your notes promptly, you will forget a good portion of the lecture material. (See Chapter 4: EFFECTIVE MEMORY. p. 35.)

Editing strategies are:

a) Find a regular time (15–20 minutes) close to the lecture to go through the notes that you took in class.

b) Set an objective for rereading.

   i) Keywords in the margin can summarize main points. This chapter models how keywords might be used.

   ii) A brief summary of the whole lecture can be a useful review tool.

   iii) Making up 2 or 3 review questions can anticipate using the material in a test situation.

c) Note down on the blank page opposite to the notes any issues that need clarification, following up on this by getting help from the lecturer, teaching assistant or colleague.

d) Add any personal reflections or expansion on the topic, also on the blank page or in "whitespace" in your notes.

e) Reread keywords (at least!) every two weeks in order to refresh your memory on course content.

You may wish to talk about the course with other students. You can learn a lot from the approach they take. It is also invaluable to find out what the instructor's perspective is on the course and the approach he/she advises if you are having real difficulties. As you will encounter many different types of lectures, your role is to find the best approach to note-taking for each one.

WARNING! ! !

Avoid recopying your notes — it uses up a lot of study time and you do not learn much because you are not actively selecting and organizing.

Margin notes:

Edit Notes Within 24 hours !!

Strategies

a. Regular time after lecture

b. Set objective:
  i). Keywords
  ii). Brief summary
  iii). Make review questions

c. Note issues to be clarified

d. Add personal reflections, etc.

e. Reread every 2 weeks.

Talk to prof & students re: notes.

Avoid Recopying Notes !!

SUGGESTIONS FOR THE 'PROBLEM' LECTURE

Check your note-taking strategies in the following examples:

1. *You are having difficulty understanding lecture material.*

   Have you a) completed assigned reading before the lecture?
   b) reviewed previous notes on the topic?
   c) asked for help after defining as accurately as possible which issue is difficult to understand?

2. *You find you can't get everything down in your notes.*

   Check whether a) you really need to record every detail.
   b) other students share your impression — can you exchange notes to fill in gaps?
   c) you can develop appropriate abbreviations.

3. *You seem to take down the "wrong" information.*

   Do you a) attend to repetition and emphasis by the lecturer?
   b) note down any summary she/he gives?
   c) use subheadings to highlight the main points?

4. *You find that you haven't reread your notes after several weeks of class.*

   Consider whether a) the lecture notes are an important feature of the course or not. If not, focus more on listening in lectures.
   b) your notes are too disorganized as a result of a lack of editing.
   c) you can schedule review time into your weekly study plan.

5. *After two or three weeks, you still can't follow the lecturer. You can't pick out what's important or where the lecture is going.*

   Try to a) attend another lecture section in addition to, or instead of, the one you are assigned to.
   b) explain the problem to the instructor to see if she/he has some suggestions for you.
   c) ask another student in the course if you can see the notes from the last lecture.
   d) talk to other students out of class to see what their perceptions of the course are.
   e) tape a lecture and listen again to the same material. Improve your original notes with this review.

EXAMPLES OF NOTE-TAKING

On the next 2 pages are samples of notes taken from the same lecture by two different students. In this lecture, the instructor showed slides and lectured, but he did not write anything down. Although both students attended the same lecture, student B has learned significantly more material and done this much more rapidly than student A. Student B is trying to follow the note-taking guidelines presented in this chapter. Specifically, student B has:

1) used more white space

2) used abbreviations

3) tried to make each phrase meaningful

4) tried to lay out the material with some organization, i.e., underlining, indenting, listening

5) spent 15 minutes shortly after class editing the notes by putting keywords in the margin, labelling the diagram, and filling in missing information

6) dated and numbered the pages

A Earthquakes

Earthquakes are of use to geologists. Today earthquakes in China ___ . Earthquakes begin at a focus and free oscillations inside the earth and surface waves can do damage. Inside waves are P and S waves. P waves pull-push type and secondary waves go slower and not through liquid.

 P and S waves

P- waves go around circumference but S- waves cannot go through liquid.

Knowledge of time of arrival of the wave can give information to geologists. There can be slight complications due to reflections of waves inside the earth

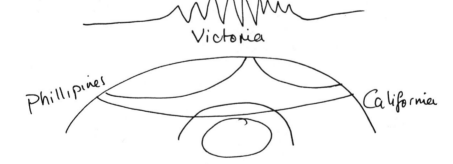

Victoria

Phillipines   California

Earthquakes	<u>Earthquakes</u>
So far...	So far earth matter in general
	Now earthquakes

Why study eqks?

Eqk of use for info about inside of Earth eg (recent)
- U.S.S.R.
- Quebec.

Eqk focus & then waves:
1.
2.
3.

Eqk focus - starts there then:
- can oscillate Earth like bell
- Surface waves cause damage
- Inside waves: P & S →
★ that's what we study here!

<u>Inside Waves</u>

Inside waves: P & S

Properties of P & S waves

Shadow zone

P waves
· push-pull
· Faster

<u>S waves</u> (secondary)
· Slower
· can <u>not</u> go thru liquid

(P waves only)
SHADOW ZONE
NO S waves rec'd
because liquid center

Time of arrival & epicenter : info
1.
2.
3.
4.

Time of wave arrival & knowl. of epicenter gives info :
1. How far thru Earth waves travel
2. Hardness
3. Density
4. Liquid or not

HOW USEFUL ARE LECTURE NOTES?

1. Monica's notes contain effective abbreviations and are a fairly concise record of lectures. In psychology, she finds that her text overlaps with her lecture notes. She would like to combine the two sources of material. *What would be the best way of doing this?*

2. Bill finds that he understands his business lecturer better if he listens carefully and does not attempt to take notes. At the weekend, he completes his record of the week's classes by using his text and remembering as much as he can. *List the ways in which he could improve his record of this instructor's classes.*

3. Jen is a very conscientious student who takes careful and copious notes throughout all her lectures. Every two weeks, she rereads them and files them away till the time of her review for exams. *How can she improve her strategy in order to make better use of her notes?*

4. Not only does Ali find it difficult to get to his 8:00 lecture in sociology, but he can't take good notes from his lecturer anyway. He decides to skip the lectures and work from his textbook instead. *What comments would you make on this approach?*

6. LEARNING FROM TEXTBOOKS

- What is a textbook?

- The role of the text in the course

- Self-assessment of current reading strategies

- Getting to know the text

- Reading strategies

- Textbook troubles

WHAT IS A TEXTBOOK?

It is important to define what it is we mean by a textbook, as approaches to reading vary much from one book to another. It is almost easier to list items that are not textbooks. For example, novels, plays, and poems in an English course are not textbooks, neither are government documents, nor research articles. Although some of the reading strategies suggested in this chapter may be of use in some instances with such materials, they often need approaches more specific to their style.

The main characteristic about most textbooks is that they are highly organized into major topics and sub-topics. This careful structuring of knowledge is highlighted by subheadings throughout any one chapter. This is especially true of modern texts in subject areas such as psychology, geography, and biology The "text structure" is carefully designed to facilitate the reading process for students. It is these structured texts that are the focus of this chapter.

THE ROLE OF THE TEXT IN THE COURSE

An important question to ask yourself as you begin a new course is, "How important is this assigned text to my learning the content of this particular course?" Usually, an instructor will talk about the textbook at the beginning of the course or will discuss it on the course outline. You will need to evaluate whether or not the text is viewed as a primary source of information, or simply as reference material for the occasional question. In other words, you need to be "cue aware" on this issue.

Some students don't make very wise decisions about the role of the text and spend hours working on tasks that may not lead to success.

> Nick had failed a psychology test. He was very upset and angry, and he threw down, on the desk, a thick wad of notes taken from the text.
>
> "I really studied for that test," he said. "I put in hours of work, made all of these notes, and my mark was 40%, well below the class average and a failing grade."

Nick had worked hard, putting in many hours of work with the textbook. However, the other side to this story was that he did not like 8:30 a.m. classes and had attended very few of the lectures in the course. The text covered only a small part of the course content; so, despite hours of studying the textbook, he was very unprepared for the test.

Think of the courses that you are taking. Probably there is quite a lot of variation in the role of the text in these courses. Identify one course and answer the following questions:

Course: _____

1. What messages has the instructor given about the way in which the text is to be used in the course?

   _____

   _____

2. How similar or dissimilar is the content of the lectures and text?

   _____

   _____

3. How important is the text to doing well on the examinations?

   _____

   _____

4. Do you have a plan for your use of the text?

   _____

   _____

SELF-ASSESSMENT OF CURRENT READING STRATEGIES

Of all the courses that you are currently taking, which would you select as your heaviest reading course?

_____

Think about that course for a moment, and in particular think about the last time that you were reading the textbook. What for you are three of the problems or issues that you were dealing with?

1. _____

2. _____

3. _____

Keep these in mind as you read through this chapter to see if you can identify any strategies that might allow you to become a more effective reader.

With your heaviest reading course in mind, complete the following inventory by checking as many of the statements as you feel represent your reading strategies. If your strategies are not present, add them in the spaces provided.

1. Time management

    a. every week, I regularly read the required pages.
    b. periodically, I catch up by reading several chapters.
    c. I only read the text when I am reviewing for a test.
    d. I never (or rarely) read the text.
    e. I read some of each chapter, but don't usually finish it.

    f. _____

    _____

2. Approach

    a. for any chapter, I just begin at the first page and read the chapter straight through.
    b. I spend some time looking through a chapter before beginning to read.
    c. I read the summary before I read the chapter.
    d. after I've finished reading the chapter, I spend some time looking over the headings again.

    e. _____

    _____

3. **Integration with the lecture**
   a. I read the chapter before the topic is covered in class.
   b. I read the chapter after the topic is covered in class.
   c. sometimes I read before and sometimes I read after the class.
   d. I check the class notes against the text.

   e. _____

   _____

4. **Concentration**
   a. I read where I won't be disturbed.
   b. I often spend 3 or 4 hours reading without taking a break.
   c. I take regular breaks after every hour or so.
   d. I have a definite goal in mind as to what I want to accomplish, and I work towards it.
   e. I daydream a lot when I read.
   f. I allow myself to be easily distracted while I am reading.

   g. _____

   _____

5. **Memory**
   a. I just read and try to remember.
   b. I highlight.
   c. I take notes from the chapter.
   d. I use the study guide to reinforce the content.
   e. I recite aloud or to myself to memorize important points.

   f. _____

   _____

6. **Exam review**
   a. I reread everything for every test.
   b. I reread my highlighting and/or my own summary notes.
   c. I reread the text summary.
   d. I use the study guide.
   e. I ask the instructor or other students about things I don't understand.

   f. _____

   _____

GETTING TO KNOW THE TEXT

Before reading a text, or section of a text, spend some time browsing through it. Find out about its background, content, and organization. Surveying can establish expectations that can positively affect both reading strategies and comprehension of the material.

Background

1. *Who wrote the text? Was it one author or several?*

If the text is written by one author, you may expect a consistent style of writing. If several authors contributed, then there may be considerable differences in style among the chapters.

2. *What information is given about the author and how does the author's perspective affect the content?*

In many disciplines, there are differing viewpoints on important issues. For example, you would expect a political commentary from a conservative viewpoint to contrast sharply with one from a liberal author. It is important for the reader to identify the approach, if possible, before reading the text.

3. *When was the text written?*

Science and technology and consequently society develop so rapidly that information and perspectives quickly become outdated. Certain types of information date more rapidly than others. You should always check the date of publication to assess the relevance of the content. This will depend on the context within which you wish to use the information.

4. *Where was the text written?*

The cultural environment within which the author was educated will have played an important role in the development of his/her ideas. In some fields of study, information is freely transmitted from one country to another, but in other cases it is not. Even when communication exists, the focus of study may differ drastically from one country to another.

The preface will often give answers to these questions that have been asked.

Content and Organization of the Book as a Whole

Look through the Table of Contents and check the chapter titles:
- what topics are included?
- what is the order of topics?
- is the book subdivided into major sections?
- what additional information is there — a glossary, appendix, index?
- how does the text match the lecture topics?

You should ask yourself, "What do I know about these topics? From my experience, can I identify with any of these topics? Do I find them interesting? provocative? depressing?"

Content and Organization of Each Chapter

- how are the chapters organized; are they subdivided into sections, and if so, can the sections be easily identified from the headings?
- how are the points illustrated: with pictures, figures, tables?
- are any keywords listed?
- are questions included?
- how are key ideas and definitions highlighted?

Look through your text and check off the items as you identify them:
- 1. author's preface to text
- 2. table of contents
- 3. chapter headings
- 4. introduction to each chapter
- 5. headings within each chapter
- 6. figures, illustrations, etc.
- 7. conclusions or summary
- 8. list of keywords
- 9. questions or problems based on the chapter
- 10. glossary
- 11. appendix
- 12. index

Before reading any one chapter, look carefully again through the table of contents at the front of the text. Check which topics are covered, and in what sequence. What is the logic behind that particular order of topics? Is the author building a case for any particular argument? How does the chapter that you are about to read link with those immediately before and after it? Each chapter will make more sense when viewed in the context of the entire text.

READING STRATEGIES

There are no right or wrong ways to read a textbook, although some general approaches work better than do others. The strategies suggested here are based on a variety of sources. First of all, students report to us the approaches that work for them. Second, the research literature reports studies on effective and ineffective strategies. Third, the authors have research in progress evaluating effective reading. The strategies are organized into:

Pre-reading strategies

Reading for comprehension strategies

Post-reading strategies.

As you read through this section, evaluate each strategy in terms of its potential effectiveness for your specific reading assignments. You will not use all of these strategies, only those that are appropriate to your needs. Your approach to reading a textbook will vary with:

- the amount of time you have to complete the task.
- the other competing tasks at that time.
- whether or not you are about to be tested on that content.
- your level of organization and interest.

Pre-reading Strategies

1. *Activate your background knowledge*

   Think about the topic and what you know about it. Recall any relevant lecture material.

2. *Survey* the following

   1. Chapter title (What does it mean? What is the chapter about?)
   2. Headings and subheadings (What are the topics and how are they organized?)
   3. Introduction and summary (What do they tell you about the content?)
   4. Captions (What is illustrated in the pictures, figures, and tables?)
   5. Bibliography (What are the extra sources on this topic?)

3. Outline the chapter

By writing down the title, and then listing all the headings and subheadings. The following outline is based on Chapter 4, "*Learning*", in the introductory text, PSYCHOLOGY, 2nd edition, (1986) by Henry Gleitman, published by W. W. Norton and Company Inc.: New York.

Chapter 4: Learning

1. Habituation

2. Classical Conditioning
   - Pavlov and the conditioned reflex
   - The major phenomena of classical conditioning
   - The scope of classical conditioning
   - What is learned in classical conditioning

3. Instrumental Conditioning
   - Thorndike and the law of effect
   - Skinner and operant behaviour
   - The major phenomena of instrumental conditioning
   - What is learned in instrumental conditioning

4. Behaviour Theory and Human Disorders
   - Behaviour therapy
   - Behaviour theory and medecine

5. Some limitations of behaviour theory
   - the biological constraints on learning
   - cognitive learning
   - the generality of behaviour theory

Summary

Reading for Comprehension Strategies

1. *Focus on a subheading*

   Ask yourself what the section is about. Not all sub-headings are very informative; but if they are, use them to set up expectations of what the section is about. For example, in the outline on page 69, the first subheading is "habituation". What kind of word is "habit"? What has this to do with the chapter title "Learning"?

2. *Pick up clues from the text layout*

   If a word is highlighted, either by bold or italicized type, then it is asking to be evaluated carefully. Diagrams or pictures need to be scrutinized as you read the text referring to them. Information separated into marginal notes, or an insert box, is there for a purpose. Look at it carefully to see what it contributes.

3. *Rephrase a sentence or paragraph into your own words*

   If you paraphrase in your own words as you read the text, you will be achieving two important goals. First you will be checking that you understand the information enough to rephrase it. Second, you will be putting that information into long-term memory.

4. *Form a visual image if the material is appropriate to that technique*

   There are many topics that are very visual. For example, in the chapter on "Learning" referred to earlier, you might try to imagine the laboratory setting where Pavlov researched the conditioned reflex with dogs.

5. *Make associations with both your general knowledge and with information from lectures and readings*

   The more connections you make between new information and knowledge you already possess, the better you will understand and remember that information. The most powerful associations are with your own experience. You need to daydream creatively as you read. You will be integrating ideas as you read and think.

6. *Respond emotionally to the content*

   Allow yourself to *feel* the text. On the positive side, get excited, thrilled, surprised, and interested. On the negative side, get irritated or angry, as long as this does not distract you from the concepts you have to learn. Emotions help you to stay motivated and to remember information.

7. *Use a selection framework to select out main ideas*

You may wish to reread pages 42–48 in Chapter 4 where this strategy is first introduced. Briefly, some of the critical types of information to look for in an argument-based selection framework are:

- *Key concepts.* They form the basis for the information. Make a list of these concepts. Some texts already do this for you, as a brief summary to a chapter. If your text does not, try to do this for yourself.

- *Definitions.* For each concept, define the idea, preferably in your own words. Especially be careful with related pairs of concepts. It is very easy to build exam questions around such pairs. For example, in "Learning" a student needs to discriminate clearly between "classical" and "instrumental" conditioning.

- *Explanation (description of key characteristics).* This is often the detailed information that most frustrates students. They say, "How can I remember all these nitpicking details?" The answer is that few people can remember them all, but they are easier to remember if you tie them to the underlying concept. If possible, try to see the logic or patterns in the details you are identifying.

- *Examples and/or analogies.* Always link an example and/or analogy back to the concept it is illustrating and ask yourself, "What does this describe about this concept?" or "Why are they using this particular example?"

- *Research questions and evidence.* Sometimes there is disagreement among experts on explanations of phenomena or events. An expert may ask questions and present evidence in support of a theory. Others will present criticisms of the argument.

- *Generalizations or conclusions.* Sometimes text leads up to some overall statement or summary. If the text does not summarize explicitly in this way, try to do it yourself. Generalize by saying, "O.K., so that was really saying ......"

Post-reading Strategies

1. *Make a record of the key information*

   If you are one of the majority of students who remember information better after writing it down, then plan to record key ideas. There is a variety of methods to choose from. Consider the following:

   - *Underline and/or highlight.* If you read to understand first, and then go back to underline or highlight, you will have more success in selecting only the important points. Avoid highlighting too much. Concentrate on the important key ideas. You may wish to develop a set of symbols for different kinds of information, e.g., brackets, boxes, asterisks, and circles.

   - *Add keywords and/or brief notes to the margin.* Again, focus on the main ideas or details for these keywords and marginal notes.

   - *Make a separate set of summary notes.* Condensed notes can save time when you review. They reduce the interference that occurs when processing too much information in too short a time period. Translate the ideas into your own phrases rather than copying verbatim. Also, read at least a page before summarizing ideas, or you will most likely take too many notes. You may find yourself re-copying the text!

   - *Develop a diagram to illustrate main ideas and relationships between them.* For some people, the more graphically the information is displayed, the easier it is to remember. This technique is sometimes referred to as cognitive mapping.

   - *Make up test questions.* If you can translate a chapter into a set of test questions, you may be anticipating the test. Trade your questions with a friend. This can help both of you.

   - *List keywords.* Go through the chapter when you have finished reading and make a list of keywords related to the important ideas.

2. *Recite the important information from memory*

This is an important step in transferring information from short-term to long-term memory. Try all or some of the suggestions.

- Cover the page. Recite silently, or out loud, the points that you just read. If you can't remember, re-check the page and try again.

- You don't need to have the text or notes with you when you recite. When you have a few spare minutes (at the bus stop, or when you are walking between classes) try to recall the organization of a chapter by reciting the headings.

- Think about the keywords list that you made. How many of those keywords can you recall?

3. *Review material and self-test*

Forgetting will be a problem if there is a long gap between learning and testing.

- Review immediately after reading a chapter in order to put it all together. This should not take long, because the information is still fresh in your memory.

- Use the study guide if one accompanies the text. Answer the questions as a review.

- Review every two weeks to integrate the material as the course progresses.

- Before the exam, plan a definite amount of time to spend in careful, thorough review.

- Self-test in as many different ways as you have time for. If old exams are available, rehearse by simulating the real test.

- Organize or join a study group to discuss the course concepts with other students.

TEXTBOOK TROUBLES?

1. Lee has been busy the first month of school with class, add/drop, residence parties, etc. He hasn't bought his textbooks but relies on his friends and uses theirs when they're finished. *Why is this a poor approach?*

2. Julie is a really serious student who reads each chapter. She always makes notes, but sometimes wonders if this is the best use of her time. *What suggestions can you offer?*

3. Melissa makes herself sit down and read at least three hours a night, reading for one course per night. In spite of all this preparation, she does not join in class discussions because she cannot remember what she has read. *Any suggestions?*

4. Alain doesn't like reading. He finds that he gets sleepy about 15 minutes after he begins. *How can he maintain a better approach?*

7. SCIENCE PROBLEM-SOLVING

- Introduction

- General strategies for problem-solving courses

- Your current approach to problem-solving courses

- Specific strategies for problem-solving courses

- A few ideas about exam preparation

INTRODUCTION

Problem-solving courses such as mathematics, physics, chemistry, and statistics, present some unique, and often difficult, challenges to the student. Consequently, the student intending to be a *good strategy user* will look for appropriate strategies to handle these courses. This chapter introduces strategies intended to improve performance in problem-solving courses. Although many problem-solving strategies have been put forward by others, the ones presented here were selected because:

a) they are fairly easy to monitor, that is you know whether you are using them or not.

b) they are not "that obvious", that is, most of these strategies are either underused or not used at all by most students.

This chapter is in two parts. The first part looks at general strategies that involve use of time and resources. The second part presents specific strategies for studying, in other words. ideas about what to do while you are studying problem-solving courses.

GENERAL STRATEGIES FOR PROBLEM-SOLVING COURSES

1) *The majority of your study time must be spent actually-solving problems.*

Many students spend far too much time reading and re-reading the text and trying to memorize formulae and solved examples. Because exams in problem solving courses require that you solve problems, you need to practise doing just that. Therefore, you should try to learn the basics of each concept as quickly as possible and then get right into solving problems. This also means concentrating on learning the basics *in the lecture* (as opposed to just copying the notes) so that you can minimize the time you need to read the text. Once an understanding of the basic concepts is reached, try to re-solve the solved examples in both the text and the lecture before starting the practice problems.

2) *Find and do harder problems (that are appropriate).*

Exams in problem-solving courses tend to focus on the harder problems in the course; so, quite naturally, your study time should reflect that bias. Not only is it important to solve quite a few problems, it is also important to solve a number of the harder problems. Harder problems often intimidate students; but, the point of this strategy is that you need to look for and to prepare the harder problems rather than avoiding them. A number of the other strategies in this chapter deal with ways of approaching harder problems.

3) *Set a time limit (usually 15 minutes) on each problem you attempt.*

This may be the most important strategy of the chapter, but it is also a very difficult one to follow consistently. Many students easily get "hooked" when trying to solve a problem, and spend one or two hours trying to "get that darn problem!" Unfortunately, if you run across a few problems like this, you could expend a lot of study time and have very little, other than frustration, to show for it. This "getting hooked" pattern is certainly an important factor in the failure of many science and engineering students. So, plan to attempt at least four problems in one hour; after the first 15 minutes (use a timer if necessary), go on to the next problem even if you are stuck on the first one. What do you do about the problems you cannot solve? The next strategy suggests some ways to get "unstuck".

4) *Develop useful help sources and use them regularly.*

When stuck on a problem, most students typically consult their lecture notes and text; but often these sources do not help. However, there are other resources such as the instructor, tutorial assistant, help centre, tutors, students, and different texts and solution books (e.g., Schaum's outline series). Good students often use a greater range of help than do less successful students. However, to use resources, you first have to locate them. Also, in order to use help resources effectively, keep track of the difficulties that you encounter. Small groups of students (2 to 4) working on problems together can also be an excellent resource.

5) *Have the necessary background and skills.*

Because many problem-solving courses, such as statistics and physics, are required for certain programs or degrees, there is a great temptation to attempt these courses without having the adequate background knowledge and skills. This makes a difficult course just about impossible. To avoid this trap, make an early investigation into any special problem-solving courses you need to take. Talk to the instructor, get a course outline or old exam, and see what kind of background is really necessary. If your background is weak, there is a variety of ways to remedy this. Many institutions have specialized learning centres that offer diagnostic testing and self-paced instruction; correspondence high-school subjects are also available in a variety of subjects; if your weaknesses are not very serious, you could try working through an appropriate text on your own.

YOUR CURRENT APPROACH TO PROBLEM-SOLVING COURSES

	Frequently	Occasionally	Rarely/Never
1. I have the necessary background and skills to handle my courses.	_____	_____	_____
2. I work on learning the basics of each concept in the lecture (vs. just taking notes).	_____	_____	_____
3. I make a prompt, brief review of my notes before the next class.	_____	_____	_____
4. I spend the majority of my study time in the course actually solving problems.	_____	_____	_____
5. I look for and attempt many of the harder problems associated with each concept.	_____	_____	_____
6. I stick to a time limit on each problem I attempt.	_____	_____	_____
7. I have developed a variety of help sources for when I'm stuck.	_____	_____	_____
8. I focus on learning & understanding the basic principle associated with each concept, i.e., crucial formulae, definitions, explanations.	_____	_____	_____
9. I carefully analyse and try to understand how a general concept is applied to a specific solved example (vs. memorizing the examples).	_____	_____	_____
10. After getting the solution to a harder problem, I reflect on what made that problem difficult.	_____	_____	_____
11. I try to predict the harder problems that are likely to appear on the exam.	_____	_____	_____

SPECIFIC STRATEGIES FOR PROBLEM-SOLVING COURSES

Three specific strategies are presented to help you study problem-solving courses more efficiently. Each deals with a separate issue crucial to success in problem-solving. These issues are:

a) learning and understanding the essential conceptual information such as definitions and formulae that is required to attempt problems involving specific concepts. (Concept Summary)

b) learning how to apply this specific conceptual information to solve the problems you are assigned. (Decision Steps)

c) keeping track of, and preparing for, the harder problems associated with each specific concept you are taught. (Difficult Problems)

The strategies presented here encourage you to write down the information associated with each of the three strategies for every concept that you are taught. At first, this act of writing down information may seem a bit awkward. However, most students who have done it consistently report that they find it more helpful and efficient than just "bashing away" at a lot of problems without any conscious or coherent summary of their efforts. Anyway, whether you write down this information or not, these three issues are ones you will have to confront in any problem-solving course.

Specific Strategy 1: Concept Summary

As in other types of courses, students in problem-solving courses need to use a framework or checklist to select the crucial information. The concept summary is such a checklist to find out what you know or don't know.

THE DETAILS OF A CONCEPT SUMMARY

For each concept you encounter, keep track of most or all of the 5 items shown below. If possible, make a brief written summary (1 page or less and in point form) consisting of, at least, the first 3 items:

1. *Formula(e) (most general and usable)*

   Usually a specific concept consists of 1 (or *a few* more) crucial formulae. All other related formulae are special cases that can be derived easily from these "first principles" so, these other formulae should *not* be learned.

2. *Definitions (including units and symbols)*

   For every new term in the formulae.

3. *Additional Important Information*

   This is information needed to apply the formulae correctly: sign conventions, assumed values, when formulae do *not* work.

4. *Explanation in Own Words/Diagram (Qualitative)*

   This is a good test of understanding. Trying to answer the question "What does this concept allow us to predict/describe?" forces you to think more deeply about the concept. Often, your own diagram or a real-life example of this concept at work can be very helpful in this regard.

5. *Proof or Derivation*

   It is often *not* necessary to learn proofs fully, as they can be abstract and time-consuming. However, some idea of a proof can be useful.

Comments

The amount of a lecture or chapter that can be considered as *one* concept is a little tricky at first. It is better to tend toward larger chunks of information for convenience. For example, the concepts of acid, base, and pH can go together as one concept rather than as three separate concepts.

Example of a Concept Summary:

Straight-Line Kinematics : Const. Accelerat'n.

<u>Key Formulae</u>:

1. $\vec{v_f} = \vec{v_i} + \vec{a}(\Delta t)$
2. $\vec{x_f} = \vec{x_i} + \vec{v_i}(\Delta t) + \frac{1}{2}\vec{a}(\Delta t)^2$
3. $\vec{v_f}^2 = \vec{v_i}^2 + 2\vec{a}(\Delta x)$.

<u>Def'ns</u>:

$\vec{v_i}, \vec{v_f}$ are initial & final velocities of object in m/s.

$\vec{a}$ is acceleration of object in m/s².

$\vec{x_i}, \vec{x_f}$ are initial & final positions of object in m.

Δt is time taken for object to go from x_i to x_f in s.

<u>N. B.</u> (additional important info):

1. $\vec{x}, \vec{v}, \vec{a}$ are vector quantities ∴ choose + direction & be consistent. eg object thrown up if up is + then $\vec{v_i} = +$ but $\vec{a} = -9.8$ m/s²

2. $g = 9.8$ m/s² <u>downwards</u>.

3. Formulae above only for const accel. eg if $x = 5t^3 \rightarrow$ no good! use derivatives!

4. When object hits ground v_f is usually just before hitting. ∴ $v_f \neq 0$!!

<u>EXPLANATION</u>: —

Formulae relate any 2 points on path of accelerating object

Specific Strategy 2: Decision Steps

Good problem-solving essentially involves making accurate decisions about the application of appropriate concepts to specific situations. It is easy to follow the instructor's accurate decisions about how to apply a specific concept to a problem; but, when you are faced with a new problem to solve on your own, it is often difficult to know where to start, i.e., What decision is first? If you are like many students, you may try to handle this situation by either plugging into formulae blindly, or trying to memorize every solution you can get your hands on. Neither of these approaches works very well. A better approach is to keep track of the "Decision Steps" you need in order to solve problems logically from first principles (i.e., Concept Summary).

THE DETAILS OF DECISION STEPS

1. *Make Decision Steps in Writing in Your Own Words*

    The steps of correctly solved examples should be carefully analysed by answering one or more of these questions for each step:

    What was done in this step?
    How was it done (i.e., which formula or guideline was used)?
    Why was it done?

    Good decision steps can clarify basic problem-solving tasks for specific concepts: identify knowns and unknowns, applying formulae as needed.

    To be most useful, Decision Steps should be brief and focus on steps you find tricky.

2. *Use and Revise Your Decision Steps*

    After you have made a few decision steps based on the analysis of a solved example, try to "test-run" these steps on a similar problem. Usually, your initial decision steps are imperfect and incomplete so revision is needed.

COMMENTS

These steps focus on the key decisions that lead to correct application of a concept, instead of focussing on the computations that result from good decision steps. Frequently, instructors will *say* in lectures what decisions they are making; but, these decisions are not written down so that students focus on the mathematical equations that are written down. Try to write these decision steps in words if at all possible. After revising your decision steps once or twice, you may want to write them down more neatly beside one or two solved examples (as shown in the example on page 83).

EXAMPLE OF DECISION STEPS: (FOR 1-D, 2 BODY PROBLEMS)

PROBLEM: A police car begins accelerating from rest at $2\,m/s^2$ in pursuit of a pair of bank robbers who are travelling in a getaway car at a const. vel. of $30\,m/s$. If the police were originally $100\,m$ behind when they started, when & where will they catch the robbers?

| STEPS | SOLUTION |

$+X \rightarrow$

1. Diag. i + f for each body

X_{ip} $\leftarrow 100m \rightarrow$ X_{iR} $\longrightarrow X_{fR}$ $\longrightarrow X_{fP}$

2. +X; origin

3. I.D. i+f info for each body (watch X_i's & signs!)

Police	Robbers
$V_{ip} = 0$	$V_{iR} = V_{fR} = +30\,m/s$
$a = +2\,m/s^2$	$a = 0$
$X_{ip} = 0$	$X_{iR} = +100\,m$
$X_{fP} = ?$ $\xleftrightarrow{\text{Same}}$	$X_{fR} = ?$
$\Delta t = ?$ $\xleftrightarrow{\text{Same}}$	$\Delta t = ?$

4. Apply this eq'n: $X_f = X_i + V_i(\Delta t) + \frac{1}{2}a(\Delta t)^2$ to each body.

$X_{fP} = 0 + 0 + (\Delta t)^2$; $X_{fR} = 100 + 30(\Delta t)$

$\rightarrow X_{fP} = (\Delta t)^2$; $X_{fR} = 100 + 30(\Delta t)$

$\therefore \Delta t^2 = 100 + 30(\Delta t)$

5. Relate X_f eq'ns of each body (usually equal)

$\rightarrow \Delta t = 33.0\,s$ (solve quadratic)

and $X_{fP} = (33.0)^2 = 1089\,m$ ⟵ check!

6. Solve & check answer/origin/signs

$X_{fR} = 100 + 30(33.0) = 1090\,m$ from where police started.

What the abbreviations in each step mean:

Step 1 Make a diagram of the initial and final points for each body.

Step 2 Choose a $+X$ direction and choose an origin (arbitrary decisions but state them).

Step 3 Identify the initial and final information from your diagram on a table as shown.

Step 4 Apply that formula using the information for each body from your table to get $X_f = f(t)$.

Step 5 Mathematically relate the equations from Step 4 (usually equations are equal).

Step 6 Solve resulting equations and check X_f values for each body. Remember your origin and watch signs.

(Making abbreviated steps for one example such as this can be very helpful.)

EXAMPLES OF DECISION STEPS MADE BY STUDENTS[1]

Problem: (N-H) and (N-N) bond energies are 340.9 kJ/mol and 158.4 kJ/mol. What is TBE and ΔH_f^o for $N_3 H_5$?

Steps & Solution:

1). *Draw structure* (check valences!).

$$\begin{array}{c} H \quad\quad H \\ \backslash \quad\quad | \quad\quad\quad H \\ \quad\quad\quad\quad / \\ N-N-N \\ / \quad\quad\quad\quad \backslash \\ H \quad\quad\quad\quad H \end{array}$$

2). $TBE = 2(N-N) + 5(N-H)$
$= 2(158.4) + 5(340.9)$
$= 2271.3 \ kJ/mol$

3). Write balanced equations for formation of molecule from standard state elements:

$$3 N_2 + 5 H_2 \rightarrow 2 N_3 H_5$$

4). Write TBE formula and solve:

$$TBE = \Sigma \Delta H_f^o \text{ atomic} - \Sigma \Delta H_f^o \text{ gaseous molecule}$$

$\therefore 2271.3 = 5(218) + 3(472.7) - \Delta H_f^o N_3 H_5$

$\rightarrow \Delta H_f^o N_3 H_5 = +236.8 \ kJ/mole.$

---

[1] The Chemistry example was made by Esther Dechant and the Calculus example by Rita Jente. Both these students found that Decision Steps helped them handle their problem-solving courses efficiently.

STEPS for SOLIDS OF REVOLUTION – DISK METHOD.

1a). Sketch curve.

b) Draw disk ⊥ to volume of revolution.

2. Find each part of disk formula: $\pi(R^2-r^2)\Delta x$.

a) R = outer Radius [upmost or right most curve]

(from line about which rotation occurs)

b) r = inner Radius [Bottom or left most curve]

c) $\Delta x = dx \rightarrow$ thickness of disk (could be $\Delta y = dy$)

d). If volume involves just one curve: subtract equation of inner radius from that for outer radius. Outer radius is usually line rotated upon.

e). If rotated about a + line (instead of axis): subtract equations for a) and b) above from that of line. (If – line add equations to that of line).

f). May need to find pts. of intersection (equate).

3. Integrate using axes that is ⊥ to disk (limits of int. given or min to max)

eg 1. $y = \cos x$. Rotate curve around $\pi/2$.

$R = \left(\pi/2 - 0\right)$ $r = \left(\pi/2 - \cos^{-1} y.\right)$

Δx here $= dy$

$\therefore V = \int_0^1 \pi\left\{\left(\frac{\pi}{2}\right)^2 - \left[\pi/2 - \cos^{-1} y\right]\right\} dy$

eg 2...

In this Calculus example the student has written the Decision Steps for the disk method above, and then applied those steps to examples below the steps.

Specific Strategy 3: Difficult Problems

Have you ever thought about what makes one problem more difficult than another? This strategy looks at some common ways to make problems difficult. The intention in doing this is to change your perspective from that of a *passive receiver* (victim) of difficult problems to that of a *strategist* who effectively anticipates difficult problems.

1. *CLASSIFY DIFFICULT PROBLEMS IN WORDS*

Try to classify each difficult problem you encounter by identifying in words (quite apart from the specific content if possible) the way or ways you feel that that problem was made difficult. Here are some common ways in which problems are made difficult (feel free to add others).

a) *Hidden Knowns:* Needed information is hidden in a phrase or diagram, e.g., "at rest" means $\mathbf{v}=0$.

b) *Multipart: same concept:* A problem may comprise two or more sub-problems, each involving the use of the same concept. This type of problem can be solved only by identifying the given information in light of these sub-problems.

c) *Multipart: different concepts:* Same idea as above, except now the sub-problems involve the use of different concepts.

d) *Multipart: simultaneous equations:* Same idea as above, except no one sub-problem can be solved fully by itself. You may have 2 unknowns and 2 equations or 3 unknowns and 3 equations and you will have to solve them simultaneously, e.g., through substitution or comparison, addition or subtraction, etc.

e) *Work backward:* Some problems look difficult because to solve them you have to work in reverse order from problems that you have previously solved.

f) *Letters only:* When known quantities are expressed in letters, problems can look difficult. If you follow the decision steps, these problems are not usually so difficult.

g) *"Dummy" variables:* Sometimes a quantity that you feel should be a known is *not* specified because it is not really needed, i.e., it cancels out, e.g., mass in work-energy problems, temperature in gas-law problems.

h) *Red herrings (extra information):* A problem may give you more information than you need. This can be unnerving if you expect to use all the given information in a problem.

2. *ANTICIPATE DIFFICULT PROBLEMS*

For each concept that you study, try to make a list of the difficult types of problems encountered as well as the difficult types that are possible and "testable" using the above list of ways to make problems difficult.

EXAMPLE OF A LIST OF DIFFICULT PROBLEMS

FOR CONST. ACCELERATION IN 1-D

I. 1 BODY PROBLEMS:

1. 1 part "simple" (eg. cyclist accelerates)
2. 1 part up-down or change direction
   (eg sandbag dropped from rising balloon).
3. 2 or more parts (eg. train speeds up
   then slows down).
4. 1 of the parts is const. vel. (eg train speeds up,
   then const. vel., then slows down).
5. Calculate avg. vel. = $\frac{\Delta x}{\Delta t}$ in these "multipart problems (eg. train previously)
6. 2 parts simultaneous equations
   eg Rock free falls & sound back up)

II. 2 BODY PROBLEMS:

1. "simple" i.e. not simultaneous (eg car &
   truck accelerate (for 3s).
2. simultaneous (i.e. equations required)
   a) Initial x's are different (eg cops & robbers)
   b) Initial t's are different (eg coconuts off cliff).

Explanation

The student here has classified all the problems she/he has seen with this concept into "subtypes" that identify important differences in the structure and difficulty of the problems. Note that many subtypes are specific examples of the *ways to make problems difficult.*

The student has also included key words about specific examples that typify that subtype, e.g., cyclist problems.

A FEW IDEAS ABOUT EXAM PREPARATION

The strategies presented in this chapter will help you to prepare effectively for exams that are involved with problem-solving courses, and to help you to avoid many of the pitfalls that have trapped so many students before. If you follow these strategies, by the time the exam approaches you will have:

a) solved a number of the harder problems (using the general strategies)

b) analysed and summarized the main concepts and how to apply them to problems (using the concept summary and decision steps), and

c) predicted possible harder exam questions (using difficult problems), somewhat like the way athletes and teams will "scout out" the opposition before the big game.

Furthermore, if you have written out the concept summary, decision steps, and difficult problems for each concept, you will have information in an "easy-to-review" format.

No matter how much work you have done, however, you will still need to do some review when preparing for the actual exam. One effective way to review a lot of problems quickly is to do *uncalculated solutions*. This means that you re-solve a few difficult problems associated with each concept by figuring out what decision steps are needed to solve each specific problem but you do not carry out the algebraic calculations, which can be quite time-consuming. Yet another useful strategy that many students use the day before the exam is to make a *formula list* on which only the "first principle" formula for each concept is shown. This list should be rehearsed frequently before the exam so that no crucial formulae are forgotten.

In addition to preparation strategies, it is also a good idea to practise specific "exam-writing" strategies as "on-exam" errors can be costly. Exam-writing strategies for problem-solving courses and other types of courses are discussed in Chapter 11: WRITING EXAMS, p. 121.

8. WRITING ESSAYS

- The challenge

- Myths about essays

- Analysing the essay assignment

- Features of a good essay

- Form of an essay

- Stages of composition

- Paragraph structure

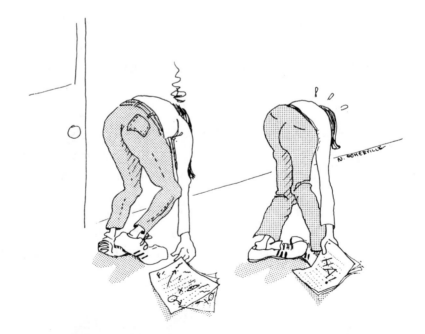

THE CHALLENGE

An essay is the product of a number of different activities such as, creating ideas, researching, planning, drafting, revising, and polishing. As most students start to write without any clear model, or ideal, in terms of a finished product, it is remarkable that so many reasonable efforts are submitted in so many courses. It is evident from student comments that they waste much time and energy, and encounter considerable frustration, as they try to express their ideas. Each paper is a challenge. However, *the good strategy user* can reconcile personal ideas with the constraints and guidelines that have been set up by the instructor. At each stage in the process of writing an essay, the student has to recognize not only what is expected but also what is possible within the available timeframe.

MYTHS ABOUT ESSAYS

a) *"You have to think up something original that hasn't been said before."*

It is seldom necessary to be original in the scope of ideas. Rather, it is important to outline your point of view and present clear evidence in support of it.

a) *"You have to make reference to all the important works on the topic."*

It's not necessary to consult every available source, or even to find that definitive review. You may limit your paper to the use of a few key items.

c) *"The longer you research, the better your ideas will be."*

Idea creation is important, but may happen fairly quickly as the result of personal experience or initial survey reading. It is important to start writing sections of the paper rather than to leave the write-up until you have done extensive reading.

The term "essay" is derived from the French verb "essayer" — to try. The essay is your attempt to express a reasoned argument, given the specifications of your instructor. No essay is ever the last word, or necessarily the best way of writing about a topic.

ANALYSING THE ESSAY ASSIGNMENT[1]

Every essay grows out of an "assignment". And nearly every assignment (whether an elaborate set of printed instructions, or a few briefly muttered suggestions from your instructor, or entirely the product of your own devising) requires that you answer certain questions before writing a satisfactory essay. Sometimes, the assignment explicitly answers these necessary questions. More often, however, you are expected to "read between the lines" and decide for yourself what kind of essay the assignment requires. These ten questions can help you to plan a more realistic approach.

1.	**Formal Conditions:**	What are the requirements of length, due date, typing, documentation, etc.?
2.	**Latitude:**	How much freedom do you have to modify the terms of the assignment — to choose your own way of answering these questions?
3.	**Subject:**	What, precisely, are you to write about?
4.	**Purpose:**	Why are you writing about this subject?
5.	**Viewpoint:**	What should be your stance as author?
6.	**The "Givens":**	What information, assumptions, and materials do you and the reader begin with in common?
7.	**Definitions:**	Are there keywords or concepts you must define?
8.	**Organization:**	What information, materials, ideas, sub-topics, questions, and answers must stand out in your essay?
9.	**Beginning and Ending:**	Is there a particular point that you must start from and/or arrive at?
10.	**Sources:**	Where can you (and where should you) get the content you need?

When in doubt, ask your instructor before you start to write. But do not ask her/him to answer the questions that appear on this list. Instead, ask for help in deciding which of your alternative answers to the questions would most likely lead to a good essay. Because you have thought about the problem, and because she/he wants to read a good essay, you will be more likely to receive helpful answers than if you ask, "What are we supposed to do?"

---

[1] Adapted from materials by Joan McCurdy, Brock University

FEATURES OF A GOOD ESSAY

1. The effective essay presents information in a cohesive and reasoned way so that the reader can follow points from start to finish.

2. It is crucial to have a statement of purpose, which is often described as the thesis, in the introduction of the essay. This thesis controls or focusses the way in which the main points of the essay are presented and developed. Therefore, every paragraph in an essay must relate directly to the chosen thesis. In the examples below, for instance, the essays associated with each of the two theses will be different, although the general topic is the same:

   a) If society takes responsibility for controlling the pollution in our environment, it may be possible to stop the depletion of the ozone layer.

   b) The depletion of the ozone layer is the number one concern for society because, unless this problem can be solved, all other problems will be meaningless.

3. Reference must be made to the literary sources that contribute evidence to the argument. Secondary sources such as a survey text, or review article in a periodical, are adequate in many disciplines. However, in some subjects the use of primary sources is required. For example, government documents or literary works, such as plays, need to be cited.

4. Sources should be woven into the argument in a clear and organized sequence. It is usually more important to maintain a clear perspective than to come up with completely new ideas.

5. The final presentation is more impressive if it avoids jargon, and uses vocabulary and sentence structure that present the ideas simply and clearly.

6. The language and style are expected to meet appropriate standards of spelling and grammatical consistency.

FORM OF AN ESSAY

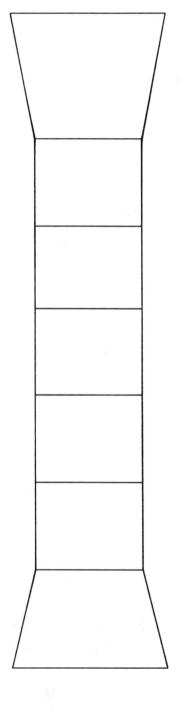

Introduction

- broad statement or announcement of subject
- explanation, detail — generation of interest
- thesis statement
- sometimes a route map outlining the subtopics is appropriate

Body

- paragraph by paragraph development of the arguments in support of the thesis
- usually four or five main points developed in paragraphs or groups of paragraphs
- points are arranged, where possible, in order of increasing importance; the strongest argument comes last; but, it is also important to begin with a relatively strong argument

Conclusion

- restatement of thesis
- possible naming of implications, wider significance
- final statement on the subject

STAGES OF COMPOSITION

1. Choosing and narrowing a topic or interpreting the question.

2. Information gathering and idea creation.

3. Formulating a controlling idea and planning a point-form outline.

4. Writing a draft.

5. Editing the draft.

6. Polishing the final presentation.

1. Choosing and narrowing a topic or interpreting the question.

a) If you have been allotted a broad topic or are free to choose one, it is necessary to *narrow* the scope to a subject that is less general, e.g.,

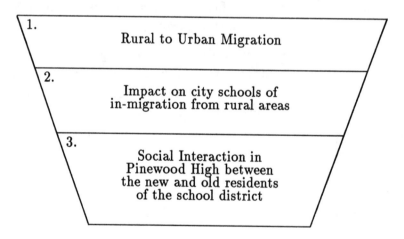

1.
Rural to Urban Migration

2.
Impact on city schools of
in-migration from rural areas

3.
Social Interaction in
Pinewood High between
the new and old residents
of the school district

b) If you are given a statement or question to consider you will have to analyse the issues, e.g., Computers will "Revolutionize" Society.

You may ask, "What kind of computers?", "What does the term 'revolutionize' society mean?", "Does the change extend to all of society or will it be limited to business, social or economic concerns?"

2. Information Gathering and Idea Creation

This is the stage of checking out different sources to find out what is available. Of course you do not have time to read everything, so it is necessary to make a decision about the most pertinent sources. Consider checking for:

a) a combination of both old and new sources,
b) a minimum number of sources, possibly 6–8, that would be acceptable; and
c) certain viewpoints that you may have noticed in lectures or discussions.

It is common for students to spend too long in this stage before making any decisions. Formulating a tentative, or working thesis, at this stage can guide the selection of appropriate information. Being able to skim and scan a variety of sources can cut down on the time needed to research the topic. Skimming through paragraphs and making brief summaries, for example, can often help to focus on the information that illustrates and explains the thesis.

Some texts will require thorough reading, and certain writing styles will need more careful tracking. As you read, it is a good idea to make notes on information useful to your topic. Interesting quotations, for example, can be key items. Some of the reading strategies in Chapter 6 will help you to gather information efficiently.

Even at this early stage, writing is very important. Take time out from reading to formulate ideas on paper. Writing and thinking are regarded by many instructors to be synonymous terms. You will not generate ideas easily without writing things down.

A note on plagiarism: This occurs when students use ideas that they have found without indicating where they found them. This often results as much from poor record-keeping as from deliberate misrepresentation.

Opinions differ about how to record all the information that you collect at this stage. As with many aspects of learning strategies, there is by no means a "best" method; but some of the suggestions that students find useful are:

i) Using index cards.

> For each book or article you locate, make a note on an index card. If you do this in proper bibliographic form, then it will be available any time you want to reference it. Adding the library call number will ensure easy access. The initials of the book will also help with indexing. On the back of the card, you can record important ideas or interesting quotations that you will be able to reference.

> *Heim, Anne*   *I & P*
>
> *Intelligence & Personality*
>
> *Penguin, Harmondsworth. 1970.*
>
> *BF 698 9I6H4   1970.*

ii) Keeping notes under different headings on notepaper.

> Allot a separate page to each topic you plan to include in your draft. Note down any relevant evidence or example on the front of the sheet, using the back for the book title.

iii) Using the computer

> If you have a computer, it is very useful to store each item of your bibliography as you encounter it. At the final write-up, you can select those that you want to include in the list of references.

3. Formulating a Controlling Idea and Planning a Point-Form Outline

Many students hesitate to move on to this stage. It is taxing to consider all the ideas collected and to devise the possible shape your final product might take. It is much easier to keep reading and recording what others have written. Many self-help books present this outlining stage as immediately preceding the final product.

However, do not underestimate how ideas begin to change and new ones "crop up" once the process of assembling your thoughts is underway. This phenomenon has been described as "thinking-through-writing", and makes the outlining phase even more of a challenge. So, although some writers claim that having an outline is very useful, others will acknowledge that they cannot predict the final structure until they have written up a few of their ideas. It may be helpful then, to refer to the "Form of an Essay" on page 93 as you proceed to this phase.

It will also be useful to be familiar with word processing as this allows you to move ideas around without writing them out again. As only one "screenful" can be seen at a time, the overall structure may be more difficult to monitor unless you print out a copy from time to time. Looking at the hard copy can also assist in making sure that editing is sufficiently ruthless. Be careful not to erase your working copy until you are sure that you have finished with it!

Being able to leave the rough outline that you initially generate for a day or so before you write up a first draft can be very helpful in allowing ideas to "percolate" before committing yourself to a particular thesis or point of view.

4. Writing a Draft

Collecting your ideas is quite a challenge, for it entails keeping your thesis in view while writing various subsections. Ideas flow much more easily if you suspend your critical self while writing the initial draft. You will have a chance to revise your composition and assess how convincing it sounds later. Because your first version will be subject to change, it is not important that each paragraph is complete as you collect your ideas.

At this point, students sometimes report being "blocked" or unable to write. Try not to think ahead to the final product but to let your ideas flow. You might even try talking them into a tape recorder before transcribing them.

5. Editing Your Draft

When you read through your draft, it is useful to have a few pointers in mind. Referring back to the original question or topic, you could ask:

a) Is the central thesis clearly stated?

b) Does the essay answer the question that was posed?

c) Does the argument stop or move off at a tangent?

d) How are the main points arranged?

e) Do all of the main points clearly relate back to the thesis?

f) Have all of the main points gathered from reading been used? If not, why not?

g) Is there material that is not clearly attached to a main idea?

You might try getting help from a neutral reader at this point. When you have become very familiar with the topic, it can be difficult to assess how quickly you can progress from one idea to another. Reading aloud to a friend can also be a way of weeding out unnecessary jargon. Check for linking words and/or sentences that indicate clearly when you move from one idea to another. These are crucial to the flow of your essay.

Furthermore	this leads to
Significantly	it is clear that
Nevertheless	the underlying factors are
Obviously	this allows for the conclusion that
And so	the following now seems obvious
Finally	all the evidence points to

Often it is difficult to discard ideas that you have carefully collected; but, if they do not add to your argument, it is better to omit them. You may sometimes be rewarded for adding points that are not strictly relevant; but, it is not a good policy to have the reader searching for your train of thought.

As you re-read, you will have to consider how the paragraphs are helping to present your argument. Further information on this and on the introduction and conclusion is outlined on pages 100–102 to assist with your editing.

6. Final Presentation

The mechanics of your writing certainly play an important role in the overall effect of your essay. Given the availability of word-processing facilities, this is an aspect of essay writing that is changing. Many institutions are now making word-processing facilities available to students. If you are not already using a word processor, take every opportunity to learn.

Though jokes are made about getting higher grades for typed papers, the issue of legibility is not a minor detail. The general appearance and layout are very important, as are the matters of correct referencing and bibliographical notation. They can help you to compose, edit, and polish your language.

References

Buckley, J. *Fit to Print: The Canadian Student's Guide to Essay Writing.* Toronto: Harcourt Brace Jovanovich, 1987.

Messenger, William E., and Jan de Bruyn. *The Canadian Writers Handbook.* Scarborough: Prentice Hall, 1980.

Modern Language Association of America. *M.L.A. Handbook for Writers of Research Papers, Theses and Dissertations.* New York: M.L.A., 1977.

Northey, Margot E. *Making Sense.* Toronto: Oxford University Press, 1983.

Northey, Margot E., and Brian Timney. *Making Sense in Psychology and the Life Sciences.* Toronto: Oxford University Press, 1986.

Paikeday, Thomas M. (ed.) *Compact Dictionary of Canadian English.* Toronto: Holt, Rinehart and Winston, 1976.

Robertson, Hugh. *The Research Essay.* Ottawa: Longparish, 1985.

Stewart, Kay, and Marian Freeman. *Essay Writing for Canadian Students.* Scarborough: Prentice-Hall, 1981.

Strunk, W., Jr., and E.B. White. *The Elements of Style* 2nd ed. Toronto: Collier Macmillan, 1972.

Turabian, Kate L. *A Manual for Writers of Term Papers, Theses and Dissertations.* 3rd ed. Chicago: University of Chicago Press, 1970.

PARAGRAPH STRUCTURE[2]

1. What is a Paragraph?

A paragraph is a group of sentences conveying a single unit of thought; that is, it presents and develops one idea only. The essay paragraph usually accomplishes these tasks:

(1) Makes an assertion (topic sentence)
(2) Explains the assertion (define, clarify)
(3) Provides evidence (details, examples, illustrations or other types of proof)
(4) Comments on the significance of the evidence

The assertion, or topic sentence, generally appears at the beginning of each paragraph. It tells the reader the exact topic with which that paragraph deals. The rest of the paragraph is devoted to explaining what that assertion means, such as defining the terms or clarifying the situation, and then defending the assertion. Further, the writer may want to explain the significance of the proof to his reader, to be sure that the reader understands why these particular kinds of proof were chosen, and therefore can judge the validity of the assertion.

SAMPLE PARAGRAPH

Topic Sentence: What seems "natural", common, and harmless in the film *Psycho* actually becomes horrid and dangerous. That is, the central features of the story — the innocent-looking young man, the quiet country

Explanation: setting, the opening detective story plot — all mislead the viewer to expect a tale about two bandit-lovers on the run. Instead, the countryside becomes a burial plot and the film records the twisted logic of a psychologically disturbed, lonesome young man. The money, for example, would ordinarily constitute the object of a vast search,

Examples: but in *Psycho*, this money becomes unimportant to the examination of the labyrinthine ways of a psychotic mind. And the common act of taking a shower becomes a horror and a disaster for the young woman

Explain meaning   as well as for the robbery caper in which she is involved. One of
of the point of   Hitchcock's purposes is thus to bring the audience to sense the un-
the paragraph: expected possibilities of disaster in our everyday routines.

---

[2] From materials by Maureen Bogdanovich, Southern Alberta Institute of Technology

2. Introductions

The introduction provides your essay with direction and interest. The reader will want to know where she/he is going and what to expect. The introduction can provide preliminary information or background observations about the subject under discussion. It sets the tone for the paper. But, generally, it should accomplish three functions:

a) announce the subject

b) interest the reader (by using apt illustrations, factors or examples — or by explaining the significance of the subject)

c) state the thesis clearly and concisely

Introductions may extend to two or three paragraphs or even two or three pages, depending on the length of the essay. Most often, a paper under 8,000 words long contains one or, at the most, two paragraphs for an introduction. The main structure of the introduction, no matter how long, is to begin with a broad view of the subject and then to narrow down to the point of your essay, the thesis statement. Generally speaking, keep your introduction as short as possible.

SAMPLE INTRODUCTORY PARAGRAPH

The Topic:	*Changing perceptions through time on masculinity, and resultant behaviour changes.*
General Statement:	What has happened to the American male? For a long time, he seemed utterly confident of his manhood, sure of his masculine role in society, easy and definite in his sense of sexual identity. The frontiersmen, of James Fenimore Cooper for example, never had any concerns about masculinity; they were men, and did not occur to them to think twice about it. But one begins to detect a new theme emerging in twentieth-century literature: the theme of the male hero increasingly preoccupied with proving his virility to himself. Today, men are more and more conscious of maleness not as a fact but as a problem.
Examples – Development of Interest:	
Thesis Statement:	There are multiplying signs indeed that something has gone badly wrong with the American male's conception of himself.

3. Conclusions

The concluding paragraph focusses the reader's attention on the purpose, thesis, and subject once again. The paragraph begins with an altered or extended statement of the thesis, and then traces the implications or consequences of the idea outwardly to broader applications. It should accomplish the following functions:

- remind the reader of the main subject and purpose
- explore the greater implications and general significance of the subject
- convince the reader of the subject's value

Several ways of ending an essay convey a sense of finality:

- a) summary of ideas with suggestions for further study
- b) personal evaluation of the presented idea
- c) appropriate quotation and comment about its significance
- d) extension of thesis into larger truth or universal consideration

Naturally, you will not use all of the above methods in a single conclusion; choose the method that seems appropriate to the subject of your paper. The basic principle is to restate the thesis, and then end the paper gracefully without introducing new material. Proportion the length of the conclusion to fit the length of the whole essay. A short paper will require only one paragraph; in a long paper, you may wish to restate your thesis in one paragraph, fully summarize your arguments briefly in a second paragraph, and discuss the significance of your argument in a third. Keep your conclusion as short as possible, depending on the length of your paper.

SAMPLE CONCLUSION PARAGRAPH

Original thesis was as follows:	**D.H. Lawrence's explicit view of the place of women contrast with his characterization of Mrs. Morel and Lady Chatterly.**
Concluding Statement:	The characterizations of Mrs. Morel and Lady Chatterly, therefore, seems to contrast with Lawrence's directly stated opinions about the relationship between men and women.
Thesis Restatement and Extension of Idea:	Perhaps Lawrence unwittingly is revealing the strange dichotomy most men hold subconsciously about women, believing rationally that women have a right to individuality but preferring them to maintain a subordinate and inferior position. If so, this unconscious desire could help explain
General Comment:	the widely evident discrimination against women in jobs, in salaries, and in status.

9. PRESENTING A SEMINAR

- How do you feel?

- Researching the information

- Structuring the ideas

- Presenting the information

- Keeping calm

HOW DO YOU FEEL?

Students vary a lot in their response to the assignment of giving a seminar. For some, the experience is an exciting challenge and an opportunity to share ideas with peers. For others, there is more anxiety than excitement, often because students have so little practice in giving presentations. How do you react to some typical student comments?

	Yes	No
1. I will be too scared to speak.	——	——
2. My biggest problem is knowing what to talk about.	——	——
3. I gave a seminar before and it was not too bad.	——	——
4. The prof usually helps out if you get stuck.	——	——
5. I really don't know what to expect.	——	——
6. Everone else in the class knows how it feels.	——	——
7. My hands always shake.	——	——
8. I'm always scared that I will go blank.	——	——
9. I don't think that it will be too bad.	——	——
10. I'm actually looking forward to it.	——	——
11. I'm scared that I will not be able to answer the questions.	——	——
12. I know that it will feel good when it is over.	——	——

Your comments?

13._____

14._____

15._____

16._____

17._____

18._____

19._____

20._____

If you have never given a seminar before, or if you are feeling anxious about the event, then in order to be strategic in your approach you need to get a clear idea of the three components[1] of a seminar presentation.

- Researching the Information
- Structuring the Ideas
- Presenting the Information

RESEARCHING THE INFORMATION

Because researching a seminar topic has much in common with researching an essay, it will be useful at this point to reread pages 94–99 in Chapter 8, WRITING ESSAYS. Good research usually results from good decisions about strategies, and so throughout this initial stage it is important to focus on some key questions.

The Content

- What is expected? Is the seminar to be a review of the literature, original experimental research, personal experience or a combination of these three?

The Topic

- Is there an assigned topic or is it your responsibility to generate an idea?
- Can you choose a topic in which you have a personal interest?
- What are reasonable limits to set for this topic?
- If you are reporting your own original work (such as experimental results), is it an interim report or a final report in which you present your overall conclusions?

Research

- How many books, journal articles or other sources of information should be referenced?
- How can you survey the information most efficiently?
- What is the best system for recording key information?
- Is there a theme or angle emerging that will give structure to the topic?

---

[1] Based, in part, on materials by Colin Baird, Educational Development Office, The University of Western Ontario.

STRUCTURING THE IDEAS

Although structuring ideas for a seminar presentation is similar in many ways to structuring of ideas for an essay, there are also important differences. The reader of an essay can always glance back to recheck previous sections if there is a problem of flow of ideas. Members of the audience cannot do that unless they ask questions during the presentation. A good seminar should have a lot of "markers" for the listener so that the *structure* comes through clearly.

Beginnings

You need to get the attention of your audience at the outset, and the way in which you do this will depend on the type of seminar that you are giving. In appropriate settings, you can begin with an anecdote, cartoon, or quotation.

For all seminars, you should clearly inform your audience on the *topic* and the *outline* of the presentation. It may be necessary for you to specify the *goals* that you wish to accomplish. Also, you may need to give some brief background to the main topic, but be careful not to detract from your major focus.

The Body

Seminars are most commonly organized around a small number of sub-themes that fit together in a structure suitable for the topic. For example, begin with facts and description, followed by explanations and examples, and finish with significance and conclusions.

Clear transitions between the subthemes will make a big difference to the ease of comprehension for the listener. Because time constraints can be very tight for many seminars, do not place your most important observations at the very end in case you have to finish in a hurry.

Endings

The ending should be well planned to accomplish a particular goal. For example, if you have to persuade your audience to a particular point of view, then summarize with your strongest arguments. Do not give the audience any ammunition, in terms of counter arguments, but anticipate the reactions and have some responses rehearsed.

It may be useful to review with the audience the original purpose for your seminar and evaluate what you have achieved. If the seminar is to be followed by a question period, then you might pose some tentative questions to be explored. Controlling the question period requires skill.

PRESENTING THE INFORMATION

If the seminar is to go well, it is important that you plan and practise the delivery. Think of it as a performance with you as the star.

Rehearsals

Practise the whole seminar aloud, in a location where you will not be disturbed. Try not to rush through the material, and keep track of the amount of time it takes. Over-rehearse the first few phrases so that they are fairly automatic and require less conscious thought as you get into the delivery. Imagine yourself in the seminar in a relaxed "positive", frame of mind. In the hour before the presentation, exercise your lips and jaw so that they feel relaxed when you begin to speak.

Check Out the Space

Check out the room for size, shape, and seating. Also, if necessary, know where the light switches and electrical outlets are located. Check equipment such as the lecturn, projector, screen, and tables, and watch for things that you may trip over.

Try out your voice in the room, and if it is a very large room, talk to the back row. You will need to practise projecting your voice to gain control over the amount of air you need. You do not want to appear breathless throughout the seminar!

Your Notes

Consider which format you prefer for notes. Are you going to use notepaper or a series of cards? Many people feel much more comfortable when they have a good set of notes even if they never use them. However, try to get away from total dependence on notes so that the audience will feel more relaxed and receptive to your presentation. Notes on a lecturn are easier to read and, as your head is up toward the audience, you will be more audible.

Take care that your notes are not in a location where they can get blown about in a breeze, e.g., from the overhead projector fan. Number the pages so that you can organize them fairly quickly if they get out of order. On your notes, include large organized headings with space in between so that if you lose your place you can find it again as quickly as possible.

Visual Aids

TRANSPARENCIES:

- Place only a few key ideas on each transparency. Most novices tend to overload the audience with masses of detail and underemphasize the key points and relationships. Remember the K.I.S.S. mnemonic: Keep it Simple, Student!
- Use readable size type. If the audience cannot read it then do not use it. If necessary, enlarge the type on a photocopier as you make the transparency.
- Handwriting must be legible.
- Use colour and/or overlays to simplify complex information.
- Give the audience time to read the basic information before adding any analysis or other additional information.
- Number your transparencies.
- Don't stand in front of the screen.

SLIDES:

- Check the equipment to make sure that it is operating functionally, and to ensure that all of the slides are inserted correctly.
- Avoid going back to earlier slides. Have duplicate slides if necessary.
- Avoid plunging the room into sudden darkness, or snapping the lights on without warning.
- Have a small flashlight on hand to check your notes.

VIDEO/FILM:

- Check your equipment.
- Avoid really long segments as this interrupts the presentation. Also make sure that the materials are relevant to your topic.

CHALKBOARD OR FLIPCHART:

- Write down main ideas only.
- The information must be readable to everyone.
- Remember that the audience enjoys reading its own contributions.

HANDOUTS:

- Handouts can divert attention from yourself.
- If the handout is to be used as an integral part of the presentation, the information should be kept short. If it is to be handed out afterward, then more detailed information can be included.

Voice

On the way to the seminar, "warm up" your voice by humming a favourite tune. Voice projection can be improved with some easy exercises, for example, to get prepared for the presentation practise saying your favourite nursery rhyme with your teeth clenched tightly shut in order to exercise your lips.

> "Mary had a little lamb, its fleece was white as snow,
>   And everywhere that Mary went, the lamb was sure to go."

In the seminar, everyone must be able to hear your presentation, and so the pace should be slower and more deliberate than for conversation. Aim for the back of the room, and look up toward the audience. Pause at the end of phrases so that the listener can follow the train of thought. Try to avoid a dry throat by sipping a glass of water, sucking a lozenge or lightly biting the front of your tongue before you begin.

Body Language and Appearance

Try to be as natural as possible. Move around a little and, if you are over-conscious of your hands, hold a pen or other aid. Wear something that is appropriate, tidy, and comfortable.

Handling Questions

When someone asks a question, repeat or rephrase it so that everyone hears the question that was posed. Take time to consider an answer, as no one one will expect an immediate response. Give credit to the questionner with a comment such as, "That is a good question."

Don't try to answer questions if you do not know the answer. You can say "That is a difficult question," or "I'm not sure that I have an immediate answer for that." On the other hand, have questions ready for the audience, and also anticipate possible questions and have some responses ready.

Feedback

Learn from the experience by asking for some feedback from friends in the audience. Ask for both positive and negative feedback so that you get a balanced view.

KEEPING CALM

Students who consciously plan their relaxation activities are often more able to handle academic stresses such as presenting seminars. When we asked students about their coping mechanisms for stress, we found that there were many different strategies used. Give each item on the following list a score to represent its use to you personally.

1 = very useful; 2 = sometimes useful; 3 = of little use

_____	1 Individual or team sports
_____	2 Walking
_____	3 Leisure-time reading
_____	4 Listening to music
_____	5 Playing the guitar, piano or other instrument
_____	6 Socializing with friends
_____	7 Watching T.V.
_____	8 Doing absolutely nothing
_____	9 Controlled breathing exercises
_____	10 Creative writing of prose or poetry
_____	11 Progressive muscle relaxation
_____	12 Handicrafts
_____	13 Going to a movie or to the theatre
_____	14 Meditation or prayer
_____	15 Using visual imagery

An Exercise in Visual imagery

Read the following scenarios and choose one of them to develop further. Relax comfortably and imagine that you are in the situation, and try to explore the most relaxing aspects of such a scene. Re-visit this scene whenever you are stressed.

1. You are on a beach at the edge of a lovely lake with the water just washing over your feet. The water is cool and refreshing and there is a gentle breeze blowing. You can hear the birds as they fly low over the water and children in the distance playing on the sand.

2. You are in a quiet pine forest with the trees stretching majestically upward. There is a faint scent of pine in the air and shafts of sunlight fall between the trees. The path on which you are walking is covered with soft, brown pine needles.

10. PREPARING FOR EXAMS

- Student comments on exams

- Where do you start?

- Important steps in exam preparation

- The final exam period

- Worried about exams?

STUDENT COMMENTS ON EXAMS

Read the list of statements on exams that have been made by students, and for each one decide if this generally applies to you or not. Put a check mark by those that do. In each case, is your answer what you think ought to apply? Add four observations of your own about exams.

1. To get down to studying for exams, I have to be in the right mood.

2. I know exactly what each of my tests is worth.

3. I don't really know how much time I should spend studying for exams.

4. If I try to plan an exam study schedule, it ends up taking a lot of potential study time.

5. It is difficult to limit the amount of study time I spend preparing for exams.

6. I tend to skip the last class before exams so that I can study.

7. Reading the text is the best preparation for any test.

8. Multiple-choice exams are tricky.

9. You don't need to know as much to answer multiple-choice exams.

10. I always do better on essay questions.

11. I try to begin writing as soon as possible in an exam.

12. Exams give me a chance to really understand the course.

13. I like to make study notes and to put all the important information together.

14. I learn much better if I work in a study group.

15. _____

16. _____

17. _____

18. _____

WHERE DO YOU START?

Randy is keen on history and would like to major in it eventually. He spends a lot of time each week reading both the text and additional readings. He takes summary notes as he reads and is confident of having a good grasp of the major topics for this test.	**Linda** has been swamped this last month with two major assignments to complete. Last, week she was sick for three days and missed several classes including history. She likes the subject but hasn't put in a lot of time and is worried about this test.

Reflect on this situation where these two students have to write a history test in three days. From the brief case studies, you can see that there is a big difference in where each will be starting the review process. Randy already has covered a lot more of the basic information and will be able to spend time reviewing material that he has studied before. Linda, on the other hand, will probably have to do a lot of reading for the first time.

Any discussion of the review process must attend to this basic fact that not all students are equally prepared. Ideally, review should be just that — review of information studied before. In our work with students, however, it is not uncommon to find students for whom review means studying new information. If this is the case, then review becomes a real challenge.

Goals for the review process will be the same for all students, regardless of background. They are:

1. To understand key concepts and important details.

2. To have good memory of the course content, and the ability to recall readily relevant information.

3. To know the requirements of typical test questions and be able to apply information in an appropriate manner.

IMPORTANT STEPS IN EXAM PREPARATION

Step 1.

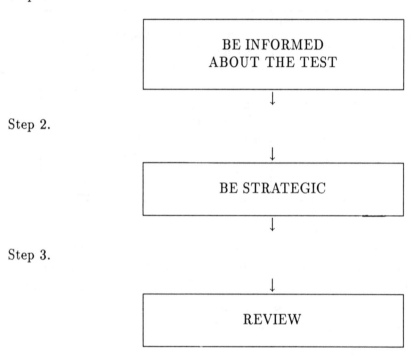

Step 2.

Step 3.

Step 1.   Be Informed About the Test

Good students take responsibility for finding out as much as possible about a test, and so some of the following questions may seem like common sense to those of you who do pick up as many cues as possible. However, not all students are good cue seekers, and that can have a negative effect on performance. For any test, you will need to keep in mind other commitments that you have and therefore the amount of time you can reasonably expect for review.

If possible, for the following questions, link them to the next test that you have:

1. When, where, and how long is the test?

_____

2. What format will be used?

_____

3. What topic areas will be covered? Are they from lectures, readings, labs, seminars, etc.?

_____

4. What special interests of the instructor might influence the topics, format, etc.?

_____

5. Are any old exams or model questions available for practice?

_____

6. What resources are available for help during the review process — instructors, teaching assistants, other students, help centre?

_____

7. What percentage of the final mark is this test worth?

_____

8. What mark do you realistically aim for?

_____

Step 2. Be Strategic

It is really important to plan your strategy of attack for review, whether you are beginning from a good base or not. There will be differences among students. For example, someone who begins well prepared can spend much more time practising the application of information to sample questions, whereas a student who has a lot of basic make-up work to do will need to fill in missing information.

1. *Set targets*. Choose your own targets in terms of content to be completed by certain dates. Setting up a plan seems to motivate many students by giving them measurable goals to aim for.

2. *Decide where to work*. Avoid settings with obvious distractions. Also, choose a place well away from interruptions by friends.

3. *Begin with content that you find most difficult.* This task in itself is difficult for some students, and they have to consider seriously which topics these are. You may need to get help during the review process if you are unclear on concepts.

4. *Plan the order in which you will go through the content.* This may be tied to the cues that you identified. It is not uncommon for the heaviest weight to be given to recently completed topics; and so, these should get special attention.

5. If you do not have time to study everything, then it is better to *know a selection really well rather than everything inadequately.* Target sections that you think will pay off most, if that is possible.

6. How are you going to *evaluate the quality of your review?* Do you have ways to self-test and evaluate your progress?

7. Are you going to study alone or with other students, and how can this be organized? *Group study can be effective* if there is a clear agenda for such meetings.

Step 3.   Review

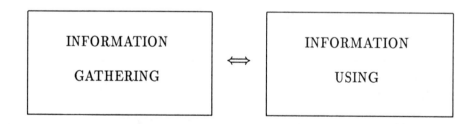

This step involves the co-ordination of two important activities. A student will switch from information gathering to information using and back again many times throughout the review process.

INFORMATION GATHERING involves reading through the sources of information for the course. Class notes are usually of prime importance as it is in the lectures that instructors highlight key concepts. Many students make the mistake of not using class notes and depending largely on the text.

The text is also an important source of information, as are your lab notes, essays, old exams, handouts — in fact all of the materials that constitute the course. Ideally, the text has been summarized either through highlighting or as summary notes, and a student does not then have to reread everything.

INFORMATION USING allows you to test your understanding of the concepts. As you review, you need to apply information in a variety of ways, and especially to create situations where you will *rehearse the test situation*. Try some of the following:

1. *Make study notes*. Outline key information by selecting important concepts.

2. *Generate new examples* to illustrate concepts.

3. *Predict questions* that may be on the exam.

4. When you think you know the information, close your books and *write or recite key information from memory*.

5. If you have an old exam available, you can *rehearse* the whole exam by using it as a trial run. Don't leave this until the last night before the exam.

6. If you are being tested through problems, as in science and economics, for example, *spend a lot of time doing problems*.

   Also — very important — review the concepts and then close your books and do the problems. You need to practise in as realistic a setting as possible, where you are drawing on memory only. This is good rehearsal for the exam. Give yourself a reasonable time limit for each question and if you get stuck go on to the next question.

7. If you are being tested through essays, again *rehearse the exam by writing short essays*. Too many students make the mistake of only reading for review when the test requires writing. Get used to recalling from memory and writing in a logical, coherent, concise manner.

8. Make up *mnemonics* for difficult-to-remember information.

   Review therefore can be seen as a two-step process, with the student interchanging the two steps throughout the review period. These two steps are:

   1. gathering in information from external sources, such as notes and text.

   2. producing information by recalling from memory and self-testing. It is this production of information that is required for exams, and that is why it is such a critical component of review.

THE FINAL EXAM PERIOD

Final exams present special demands because often a student is studying for several courses over a limited time period. This involves assessing the total picture and making some major decisions on when, and how long, to study each course.

A major trap often occurs when students overstudy for the first exams, and then running out of time and energy for the later ones. Much will depend on how the exams are spaced. Can you answer the following questions?

1. How many exams do you have and when are they? Mark the dates on the calendar on the next page and see how they are spaced.

2. What course content does each exam cover?

3. What is the format for each?

4. What percentage of the final grade is each?

5. In terms of amount study time required, can you rank each in terms of:
   1. a lot   2. average   3. little.

Courses	Material covered	Format	% of final grade	Rank

MARCH

S	M	T	W	T	F	S

APRIL

S	M	T	W	T	F	S

MAY

S	M	T	W	T	F	S

WORRIED ABOUT EXAMS?

1. Jeff is worried about a major exam he has to take tomorrow morning at 8:00 a.m. He sets his alarm to get up at 5:00 so he will have an extra 2 hours to read one more chapter. *Will he be spending his time in the best way?*

2. Sarah has a 15% term test in her 9:00 class and would like some more review time. The instructor in her 8:00 class is returning a major exam, which he plans to discuss with the class. Sarah decides to skip her 8:00 class to review for the 9:00 test. *Has she made the best decision?*

3. Mark is proud of his notes taken in Psychology 020. He plans to spend 5 hours reviewing them to ensure a high mark. His friend, Les, has just phoned him and wants to review with him. Mark accepts. *Should he have done so?*

4. Sophia knows that she has difficulty in exams in recalling key points. *How can her review be organized so that she does this more easily?*

11. WRITING EXAMS

- The exam format

- Multiple-choice exams

- Essay questions in examinations

- Problem-solving exams

- Test anxiety — good or bad?

- Can you advise?

THE EXAM FORMAT

There are many types of exam -question formats, for example: multiple choice, essay, problem solving, short answer, true/false, matching pairs, fill in the blanks. Each type of question presents demands for the student who must devise matching strategies. In this chapter, we will examine strategies for three commonly used formats:

1. multiple-choice

2. essay

3. problem-solving

MULTIPLE-CHOICE EXAMS

Students vary a lot in their response to being tested through multiple-choice exams. Some report that they prefer them to essay exams because the question stimulates considerable recall. Knowing that the correct answer is on the paper reduces anxiety for some students, and thus there is less danger of "going blank".

Other students are very fearful of multiple-choice exams. They report that the questions are tricky, out to catch you, and that it is impossible to choose between at least two seemingly right answers. It is not uncommon for a student to say, "I really knew my stuff, but I had such a hard time with those answers. The mark that I got does not reflect what I knew." Once a student begins to think this way, then high levels of anxiety can make future exams an even more difficult ordeal to face. It can be very useful to try out as many multiple-choice exams as possible in relaxed conditions to become more familiar with the format.

In our work with students, we do a lot of "error analysis" with multiple-choice exams. This involves working closely with a student, getting him/her to re-process questions answered incorrectly on the exam, and also checking source materials such as the text, lecture notes, and exam study notes used by the student for review. We work together to answer the following important question.

Why Do Students Get Questions Wrong on Multiple-Choice Exams?

1. *PREPARATION PROBLEMS*

The student does not know enough accurate information to answer the question. The most usual reasons for this are:

- *Too little time spent in review.* Some students are either so busy with other activities, such as a job, sports or social activities, that studies really suffer. It may take some negative feedback through poor test scores for a student to re-evaluate priorities and allot more time to study. However, one should be very careful about automatically assuming that the problem is quantity of time spent studying. Poor results are often more a problem of quality of studying or inappropriate choice of course.

- *Incomplete or inaccurate information.* Sometimes students are correct when they report that they really know their stuff. However, evaluation of their class notes from which they have studied can typically reveal severe underlying problems of poor note-taking. If a student takes poor quality notes in class, then that is a real impediment to further learning. Another problem may be that a student has difficulty arriving at full understanding of basic concepts   This is a difficult problem for a student, as poor exam results may be the first indication that he/she is on the wrong track.

- *Ineffective review techniques.* Many students review by reading and re-reading their lecture notes and highlighted text. This is an ineffective way to review for most exams. Effective review involves the use of active learning strategies including: attention to headings, summarizing key points using a selection framework, and reciting summaries using the headings as cues.

- *Inappropriate products of learning.* A student may have memorized by rote instead of by understanding the ideas. Although some questions on an exam may require straight recall, many go beyond this. In particular, students who do poorly may have problems with:
  1. applying concepts to a variety of examples, and
  2. making inferences from basic information, and
  3. transferring concepts to new contexts.

2. *IN EXAM ERRORS*

In this situation *the student does know the content* and can process the question accurately, but this did not happen in the exam. This may be because:

- *Anxiety* interferes with thought processes causing confused or impoverished thinking.

- The student may be trying to *speed* through the exam, not allowing for adequate time to think carefully.

- *Mistakes* can be made in the mental representation of ideas. The student may not properly interpret some of the statements.

- The student may have *inefficient test-taking strategies*, that is, the overall approach to answering questions may lead to problems.

CONCLUSION

There is no quick fix for students who experience preparation problems for exams. They may need to re-evaluate themselves in terms of *the good strategy user* and work to improve their overall approaches to learning. At this point, we will turn to the strategies used within the exam itself by asking the question, "How can students, who really know their course content, reduce in-exam errors?" The answer suggests two possible approaches:

1. Process questions systematically.
2. Stay calm — practise stress-management techniques.

A System for Answering Multiple-Choice Exams

1. *COVER UP THE ALTERNATIVES*

It is too easy to fall into the trap of reading everything very quickly before carefully reading the question. There are two dangers here. The first is that a student can become overwhelmed by the quantity of information to be processed and can panic. Secondly, much of the information that is to be processed is in the form of incorrect statements. These can interfere with existing knowledge and leave the reader confused. Use a computer card or a ruler to cover up the alternatives while reading and processing the question.

2. *READ THE QUESTION*

First of all, read to get a **general** idea of what the question is asking. If a question is very short, you may be able to arrive at a complete understanding with the first reading. However, with longer questions, the first reading may result in a general understanding of the type of question, and a student will need to go back to re-process the question again.

3. *PROCESS THE QUESTION*

This is the crucial step of arriving at a precise and **accurate** understanding of the question. Depending on the level of difficulty, you may **need** to:

- underline key words
- name the *concept* from which the question is derived
- rephrase (translate) the question into your own words

caveat — This is where many problems begin, with insufficient care applied to decoding the question.

4. *PREDICT A POSSIBLE ANSWER*

This may be possible if the question is complete in itself, and you are able to recall the appropriate information from long-term memory. Even if a question is incomplete without the alternatives, recall that general content area and especially identify the concept with some of its associated key ideas.

caveat — This is another major stumbling block. Many students do not make use of the knowledge they have. There can be a tendency to **believe** that the correct answer will "hit you in the eye" as you look at the alternatives. This is not so — you need actively to recall the relevant information.

5. *CHECK THE FORMAT OF THE QUESTION*

In some questions, there are combination answers, such as: both a) and b); all of the above; none of the above. You need this information to guide your reading of the alternatives. You will need to know whether you can respond positively to more than one of the alternatives.

6. *PROCESS EACH OF THE ALTERNATIVES*

Read each of the alternatives for meaning, not just to recognize familiar terms or phrases. Essentially, each alternative is a true/false statement about the question, and you need to respond in each case with:

√ — I think this is true
× — I think this is false
? — I'm not sure at this time

caveat — There are some pitfalls for unwary students with this step. Although exams will vary from instructor to instructor, there are some pitfalls that seem common to many. Do not get trapped by:

- *Jargon*
  Sophisticated terms catch students. They may think that a word or phrase that sounds impressive must be correct, even if in fact it is a nonsense phrase made up by the instructor.
- *Familiar phrases from the course*
  A student who "recognizes" rather than thinks through an answer may get caught by a statement that was learned in the course, but which does not answer the question.
- *Logically correct statement that is part of your general knowledge*
  Instructors know some of the myths that are part of our general knowledge, and may build them into a test question to identify the unprepared student.

7. *IDENTIFY THE CORRECT RESPONSE*

If you understand and have a good memory of course content, and have processed the question and the alternatives correctly, then the next step is to circle the correct response. However, life is not always so simple and there may be a need for some backup strategies.

8. *RE-READ THE QUESTION*

This might be where the problem lies. If not, it still makes sense to re-read the question, as there will have been a lot of processing since that first reading.

9. *ELIMINATE WRONG ANSWERS*

If you still have problems with the question, try to reduce the number of alternatives by eliminating any that seem to be obviously incorrect choices.

10. *GUESS*

This is the last resort when all else fails, and only to be used if there is no penalty for incorrect responses. With all the processing that has occurred, this will be an educated guess rather than a stab in the dark!

Sample Multiple-Choice Questions[1]

Each of the following questions has been chosen to illustrate specific points. The correct answers are indicated by arrows.

1. If a wolf or dog rolls onto its back like a puppy, we are probably witnessing
   a) a threat display
   b) a sexual display
   c) ritualized combat
   —→d) an appeasement display

This question is complete in itself, and a well-prepared student would be able to predict *appeasement* without having to read the alternatives. Note that the concept is in the alternatives and the question itself is an example.

2. Psychologists have often pointed to the similarity between territoriality in animals and personal space in humans. Available information suggests that personal space patterns in humans
   a) are instinctively determined in much the same way as in other animals
   —→b) are probably more a function of cultural and social factors than genetic determinants
   c) are very similar across cultures and societies
   d) are as predictable and automatic in humans as are territorial patterns in other animals

This question has quite a bit more reading than question one. Here the concept of *territoriality* or *personal space* is up front in the question, and the answer contains an explanation of this concept. Because one would know many things about this concept, it is not possible to predict the answer. However, it is important to define the concept and to recall some relevant information before reading the alternatives.

---

[1] Reprinted with permission of the Psychology Department, U.W.O.

3. The "cupboard theory" holds that mother-infant attachment is based primarily on fear of losing the individual that satisfies the infant's bodily needs. Which of the following observations, if true, would *support* such a theory?

- a) even when well cared for, children display intense separation anxiety upon separation from the mother
- b) children often display attachments to individuals who have not been caretakers
- →c) infant monkeys form the strongest attachments to surrogate mothers that supply food, regardless of the physical characteristics of the surrogate
- d) there appears to be no reliable difference in the quality of attachment of a human child to mother or father, no matter which of these is the primary caretaker

This question contains a precise definition of a theory. It requires knowledge of the "evidence" in support of the theory. The main pitfall in this question is that all three of the incorrect responses are true in many instances. However, they are not always true whereas the correct alternative is.

4. Suppose you lived in a culture in which people tended to be ashamed and confused about eating rather than sex. Such people might cover their faces and express shock at the sight of another person's lips. They might also limit their intake of food to unappetizing pellets hurriedly consumed behind the locked doors of small private cubicles. In such a society, which of the following statements would be most likely to be uttered by a person displaying projection, as defined by Freud?

- a) "As an artist I am best known for my portrayals of pineapples and swiss chard."
- →b) "I always notice Edith's devouring eyes."
- c) "Sure I subscribe to *Gourmet* magazine. Its articles on current events are excellent."
- d) "Yesterday I saw a truly disgusting sight — a huge roast turkey awash with rich brown gravy and cranberry sauce sitting beside a juicy apple pie. I tell you, it just about made me sick."
- e) "I was so angry with my Dad last night, I called him a 'baked potato' right to his face."

The examinee is being tested through an analogy. The concept of *projection* is applied within a new context. An essential ingredient to success is the student's ability both to identify and define the underlying concept, and then to apply it to a new setting.

ESSAY QUESTIONS IN EXAMINATIONS

Writing an essay within a short time frame (usually less than an hour) is a very different activity from composing a research essay. Usually, the objective here is to demonstrate to the examiner that you have a certain amount knowledge of the course material. Thus, most students are potentially using the same "data base" of memory, and the major skill required is the ability to answer the question succinctly, bearing in mind key priorities of the course content.

This sounds easier than it is, and, even though for many students this may be a difficult task, yet it is unlikely that many students practise this activity outside of the times that they are obliged to do so. Just as any sports performance would suffer from lack of training, so do the efforts of many a student to produce a brief, but comprehensive analysis of an essay question.

Common Problems with Essay Exams

Faults that are often criticized are:

1. Not analysing the question carefully enough to decide what key issues are involved. In other words – not answering the question.

2. Not making it clear how the essay will proceed, especially as regards overall theme. That is, there is no guiding information for the reader.

3. Not attending to how each piece of information fits with the introduction so that the end product lacks organization and relevancy.

4. Not using the vocabulary that is specific to the discipline. The language is that of everyday conversation rather than that at an academic level.

5. Not giving specific examples to illustrate general comments that you make. It is the use of appropriate examples that really confirms knowledge of a concept.

Each of these problems can be related more to the need for giving some thought to the topic than to a lack of content information. Within the time limits of an exam, attending to these problems can require deliberate planning. It is hard to: (1) survey the questions, (2) make a reasoned choice, and (3) plan a time frame for your answers while your colleagues are already scribbling furiously; but these three steps are a fairly safe bet for good results.

Effective Strategies To Try

1. As you read through the questions, jot down a few words and phrases. This will cue you to how easy or how difficult it is to recall relevant information for that question.

2. Look through the comments that you jotted down. This will help you to choose which question to answer.

3. Make your decision, and allot the time available for each essay — leaving a few minutes at the end of the exam for a final review.

4. Plan a point-form outline for each question consisting of:
   1. A re-statement of the question,
   2. The points of the content to be considered in order (ideally, one to each paragraph), and
   3. The main point you wish to make, along with any source or name you wish to quote.

   This is something that you can practise with one or two friends before the test. If you set up a few questions for each other and try to make such outlines (say four in an hour), then you can compare notes. This will improve your knowledge, as well as raise the level of your skill in planning exam answers.

5. Write your essay in a standard format (see Chapter 8: WRITING ESSAYS). Remember that you are writing for someone else to read and so your handwriting needs to be as legible as possible. If there is a problem, write on every other line. Also number your questions clearly in the margin as it is very frustrating for the marker to have to search for the beginning of your essay.

6. Finish on a positive note, even if you have doubts about having done justice to the topic.

7. When you finish the exam, if you allow some time to read over your answers to check for spelling and legibility, you may be rewarded by your reader for making the reading of your essay a more enjoyable experience.

Terms Commonly Used in Essay Questions

1.

> COMPARE AND CONTRAST significant aspects of the role of the President in the U.S with that of the Prime Minister in Canada.

Students will recognize "compare and contrast" as one of the most widely used phrases in exam questions. It is also one that is often poorly handled. It requires that points related to similarities and differences be discussed. A common problem is for students to write everything they know on the President, followed by everything they know about the Prime Minister. That is not acceptable and a student must attempt an integrated discussion throughout the paper.

2.

> ANALYSE THE SIGNIFICANCE of Canada's natural water-ways to the early settlement of the country.

This calls for something beyond a simple descriptive inventory of this aspect of Canadian geography. A student would need to discuss important concepts such as barriers, natural routeways and their potential hinterlands, resources, trade, and politics.

3.

> CRITICALLY EXAMINE the role of United Nations peace keeping forces from 1970 to the present day.

This type of question requires hard evidence for points that are made. The student would need facts, and would have to evaluate real causes, events, and consequences, as well as generating hypotheses of other possible outcomes.

These three commonly used terms are examples of a whole range of vocabulary used on exams. What is your understanding of the requirements for the following terms?

assess	describe	explain	justify
argue	discuss	evaluate	predict
define	examine	illustrate	prove

PROBLEM-SOLVING EXAMS

The third type of exam format is that of the problem-solving exam, in which you must make logical decisions that lead to a correct answer, e.g., mathematics, physics. As with any exam format, it is worthwhile to use some problem-solving exam strategies. The strategies presented here are intended to help you to avoid some of the more common errors that students make when writing problem-solving exams.

1. **Budget time to marks**. Many students get "hung up" on problems that are not worth very much. To avoid this, check the marks distribution at the start of the exam so that you can pace yourself appropriately.

2. **Read over all the problems first**. This strategy has two important advantages over just "jumping in" to solve problems. First, you can decide which questions are easier for you, and second, difficult problems can incubate in your brain while you do the easier problems. *caveat* — Only use this strategy if reading over the exam does not make you nervous.

3. **Start with the easier questions**. Often certain types of problems seem easier to you than others. By reading over the exam (or a few of the initial questions) and then starting with one of these easier problems, you can build your confidence as you write the exam. Also, you are ensuring that you are doing the problems you know how to do before tackling the more difficult ones.

4. **Minimize "dumb" mistakes**. Here are two suggestions for lowering the frequency of these annoying problems:

   a) Practise writing neatly and one step at a time. So many errors are caused by not following these guidelines, both when studying and in the exam.

   b) Monitor the "dumb" mistakes you make while studying. Some mistakes occur in the context of the problem types. By noticing that you seem to make errors in specific types of problems when you study, you can be on the alert for these on the exam.

TEST ANXIETY — GOOD OR BAD?

Many students report that they feel tense before an exam, and there is evidence that 15% of all students do less well because they cannot control their emotional response to being tested. The exam result, therefore, may not reflect their ability, or the amount of preparation they have done, or coincide with their standard on term work, assignments or essays in a course.

Symptoms of tension such as stomach upsets, headaches or rapid heart beating can be so distracting that it becomes difficult to focus on the task at hand (i.e., analysing the questions on the exam). Worry thoughts can interfere with the attention required to deal with the exam. Such thoughts as "If only I had prepared better ... This test is going to be too difficult ... What if I mess up like last time?" can take priority and, in extreme cases, result in a situation where a student goes blank, and is unable to start the exam.

Not all anxiety is negative, however. Being "keyed up" can help gather up the energy needed to achieve concentration and to be able to work through an exam paper. Research indicates that those students who are moderately nervous achieve best results.

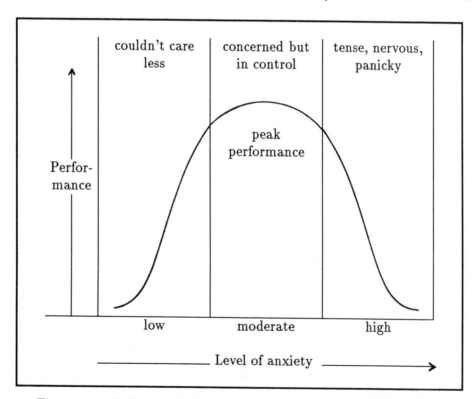

Figure 10.1 Relationship between anxiety and test performance

Controlling Anxiety

One situation in which worry can become a serious problem is test-taking. This requires a student to focus on one particular issue without being distracted by doubts about performance. University and college students write many tests before they graduate. It is therefore necessary to keep these tests in perspective, and to try to see them as steps on the ladder to success rather than as stumbling blocks.

Most students feel some natural anxiety, and may need to practise conscious strategies in order to control their response to testing. It is best to plan ahead to control test anxiety rather than to be surprised by losing concentration in a test.

If your potential level of anxiety is very high, you should check with a counsellor. There are techniques for controlling anxiety that have been helpful to many people. They include systematic desensitization, relaxation or restructuring thoughts about responses to evaluation. Such techniques require time to learn and to practise so that they are not a last-minute fix.

SEVERAL DAYS BEFORE THE TEST

1. *Rehearse for the test in a variety of different ways.* Chapter 10: PREPARING FOR EXAMS explains several steps in exam review. These stress the idea of rehearsing for the event so that you will be familiar with the type of questions that will be on the exam.

ON THE DAY OF THE TEST — BEFORE THE EXAM

2. *Be as well rested as possible* before taking a test. A sound night's sleep is essential to good performance for most students. "All nighters" or studying until the very last moment are risky.

3. *Know exactly where the exam room is*, what time the exam begins, and as much about what to expect of the exam setting as possible.

4. *Get there in good time for the exam*, but do not be so early that you have to wait around. Avoid discussing content with other students. It is likely that you will begin to panic if you suspect they know more than you do.

5. Some students like to *take along a lucky charm* — a favourite sweater, pack of gum, picture of your best friend or rabbit's foot!

IN THE EXAM ITSELF

6. *Take some deep breaths* as you go into the exam room, choose your seat, and look through the paper.

7. Try to monitor signs of physical tension. *Stretch some muscles* if you sense that you are tense. Don't be shy — lots of people stretch legs, arms, and fingers in exams.

8. *Use visual imagery* to calm yourself down. Close your eyes and "see" yourself writing the exam and doing really well — suitably relaxed.

9. *Focus on positive thoughts* rather than on negative ones. There is a lot of evidence to suggest that we have a lot of personal control of **anxiety** through our "inner talk". The following four techniques help to control stress. If you can learn to use them when you are not under exam pressure, then it will be much more likely that you will be able to apply them successfully when you are in an exam.

   - **Keep your attention on the present**. Avoid thinking of past mistakes or future plans that might involve imagining negative consequesnces at a later date.

     "What's involved here?"
     "What's the next step?"

   - **Concentrate on your own approach to answering questions**. Don't get involved in watching other students in the exam or comparing their effort to your own. You have no control over other students; so, it is a waste of time to worry over their performance.

     "What do I know about this topic?"
     "What is the question asking?"

   - **Keep moving through the question**. Try not to judge your own effort by criticizing the way you are handling the questions.

     "Now I'll see what I can do with this one."
     "How does the next one look?"

   - **Control your response to test items**. Avoid generalizing about the experience by entertaining thoughts about how dumb you must be or how you don't do well on tests.

     "What did we learn about this in lectures?"
     "Well I don't have to get all the items correct."

10. Don't be afraid to stop and *take a break* during a test, especially if you regularly do that when you study.

11. *Plan a treat for after the test.* Meet a friend, watch T.V. or go to a movie. This will give you something to look forward to as you write the test.

CAN YOU ADVISE?

1. Matthew turns the first page of the multiple-choice exam paper and begins to panic as all of the questions are from the chapter that he did not have time to read. *What can he do to stay calm?*

2. Leila is just about to begin the last essay question worth 20% of the exam. She looks up to check the time and finds that she only has 5 minutes left. *What can she do in 5 minutes?*

3. Scott is about to write a history question on twentieth-century Canada. He knows so much about this topic that he doesn't know where to begin. *What should he do?*

4. Paula is feeling tired. She studied really late last night for this test, and she can hardly keep her eyes open. *What can she do to improve her energy and concentration levels?*

12. CAMPUS RESOURCES

- Getting to know your campus

- Basic resources

- Academic support resources

- Other support resources

GETTING TO KNOW YOUR CAMPUS

Modern campuses are often large, and contain a vast array of services for students. A recent survey of one university campus revealed that there were thirty-one separate directors responsible for departments providing direct student services. Probably this is not an unusually high number. Therefore, a major problem for an incoming first-year student is that it takes time to get to know all of these services.

As a first-year student, don't expect to find everything in the first few weeks. However, your experience in post-secondary education will be enriched if you are strategic about exploring ways of using the wide variety of campus resources that are available to you. Some typical campus resources are listed here under three broad categories:

1. Basic resources
2. Academic support services
3. Other support services

BASIC RESOURCES

1.1 Official Academic Calendar

This document is extremely valuable. It contains admission requirements, courses of study, descriptions of every course offered, graduation requirements, rules and regulations, phone numbers, addresses, etc. Usually, the calendar is mailed to you when you are accepted for admission; but, if you wish to look at the calendar before then, it will be available in the library or guidance centre.

1.2 Admissions Office/Registrar

Institutions usually give an approximate date by which you will be informed about admission. If you have not heard anything by a week or two after this date, contact the Admissions Office to discuss the situation.

Once admitted, you will be given instructions on registering for the courses you will take. Institutions usually designate admission or academic counsellors to help with this process.

1.3 Orientation Sessions

Most colleges and universities are fairly large operations employing many people, in a variety of departments, located in many different places. Finding out about services and locations can be overwhelming at first.

To help incoming students adjust to this new environment, most institutions offer orientation programs that include features such as an overview of the various student services, a look at some learning resources, and a campus tour. These programs are most worthwhile because knowledge of your campus will allow you to settle in and solve problems far more efficiently.

1.4 Housing

Often, going to college or university requires finding a new place to live for the academic year. Most institutions have a housing department, the purpose of which is to help students arrange suitable accommodation. If a college does not have on-campus residences, the housing department tends to focus on locating accommodation in the neighbouring community, including rentals, shared facilities, and boarding arrangements.

Universities typically have on-campus residences; so, their housing departments include both on and off-campus services. Establishing a good home-away-from-home is important and involves a variety of factors: location, transportation, personalities, lifestyle. If you need to find housing, discuss this as soon as possible with the housing personnel. The phone numbers for housing and other services are usually in the calendar.

1.5 Financial Aid

For many students, the cost of post-secondary education is a major stumbling block. Most institutions have a financial-aid office to help students to work out ways of affording an education. Besides the usual government assistance, this monetary aid can take a variety of forms such as bursaries, grants, scholarships, and work-study plans. If finances are a concern, contact the financial-aid personnel.

1.6 Services for Disabled Students

Students with special needs should check with the admissions office to find out what services are offered at an institution. More and more campuses now have a counsellor or department with a mandate for providing services for the disabled.

1.7 Parking

If you wish to park a vehicle on campus, you will most likely need an official parking permit and decal for the vehicle.

ACADEMIC SUPPORT RESOURCES

2.1 Instructors

Instructors can provide excellent help if you make the effort to see them at an appropriate time, for example, in their office hours or if you make an appointment. Surprisingly, many course instructors report that few students make that effort and thus their office hours are often quiet (except for a day or two before an exam!). Most instructors have a genuine interest in your learning. By preparing fairly specific questions ahead of time, you greatly increase the likelihood that the instructor will provide you with useful help. At college and university, most instructors expect you to work hard at learning the course material and so most will *not* welcome students who want the material "re-taught".

2.2 Learning Centres

For some specific courses or skill areas, academic help may be centralized in one location called a learning, or help centre, for example, the Biology Help Centre, Writing Centre or the Math Centre. Some learning centres are very sophisticated with a wealth of resources and many trained staff, whereas others are very modest with few staff and resources. No matter how well appointed, a learning centre can be a valuable academic resource, especially if you follow these three guidelines:

a) Get to know what is offered. Often the learning centre has more resources than meets-the-eye, so ask. There may be files of old exams, tutorial worksheets, videos, etc.

b) Find a staff member whom you like. Often learning centres hire quite a few staff who work part time. By meeting as many staff as possible, you can find the one or two individuals with whom you can work most effectively.

c) Use the centre frequently. Learning centres are always crowded just before exams and so the help you receive at that time is necessarily brief and rushed. A better approach is to use the learning centre regularly to clear up difficulties as they arise.

2.3 Computer Facilities

As society has become more computer literate, many campuses now provide computing facilities for students to use outside of a course. These facilities are usually fairly inexpensive for students, and it is very worthwhile to take advantage of them. Essays and assignments look better and are more easily revised using a computer.

2.4 Libraries

One of the backbones of any post-secondary institution is the library or even the network of libraries. Learning to use the resources of the library is an integral component of many courses of study. Fortunately, most libraries have the same basic features and, once you learn these features, finding your way around a new library can be easy. If you are not familiar with the following features, try to arrange for a guided tour of the library facilities. Such tours are common on many campuses.

a) The catalogue

b) The stacks

c) The reference section

d) The reserve/heavy demand section

e) Periodicals

f) Government documents

g) The on-line computer search facility

h) Films and videos

i) Inter-library loan

j) Special collections

2.5 Learning Skills Counsellors

In an increasing number of institutions, there is at least one counsellor whose main function is to help students learn more efficiently. Usually, these counsellors offer presentations or workshops on specific learning strategies related to tasks such as lecture note-taking, essay writing, text reading, and time management.

Often, they also meet with students on an individual basis to look at specific learning problems. Keep in mind that you do not have to be failing to see a learning skills counsellor. Essentially, if you are interested in improving your learning strategies, then see a learning skills counsellor.

2.6 Tutoring Services for Course Content

If you run into fairly serious difficulties with a course, it may be useful to acquire the services of a tutor. The trend on most campuses is to centralize the services of tutors; so, check to see if your school runs such a service. If not, then ask your instructor or departmental office for the name and number of a recommended tutor. Also, tutors advertise on notice boards, in classified ads, etc., but you should check with an instructor or department to find out if a specific tutor is reputable. Keep in mind that, because you are paying for the service, it is a good idea to identify clearly the specific areas in which you need help.

2.7 Other Students

This is a resource that you may underuse, particularly if you find yourself in a very large class where it is often difficult to make close friends. Make an effort to make contact with a few people in each of your classes. With your classmates, you can clarify course material, compare notes, solve problems, and work in study groups. Also, talk to students who have already completed the course as they may have useful advice and material, assuming that the course has not changed significantly since they took it.

2.8 Self-Help Books

This book is a good example of a self-help book that can help you to re-examine your approach to learning. There are other types of additional texts that can also be useful. In a course in which you are experiencing difficulty, it is a good idea to have a collection of alternate texts to check for specific explanations. The library is a good source for such additional texts.

The *Schaum's Outline Series*, containing many worked examples of problems, is a useful (fairly inexpensive) resource for courses in math, physics, economics, and many other problem-based disciplines. *Cole's Notes* is an old standby for many students of English Literature, although beware, as many instructors can readily recognize such widely available analyses. Also, plagiarism is a very serious offence; so, be very careful in the use you make of such a resource.

OTHER SUPPORT RESOURCES

3.1 Student Health Services

Students sometimes have health problems. Not only is it more convenient to have a student health centre on campus, but the health-care workers in such a facility are very familiar with the health problems typically encountered by students. You should note that Student Health Services, as with all Counselling Services, are confidential. No one, including your family, has access to any personal information without your consent.

3.2 Career-Related Resources

Most students cite career opportunities as one very important reason for pursuing post-secondary education. Career counselling helps students to explore career interests and opportunities, including the planning of both summer part-time and permanent employment. Although many students do not visit career-counselling services until shortly before graduation, you may find that a visit in your first year can be a very worthwhile experience.

3.3 Personal Counselling

Unresolved personal problems often result in considerable stress and worry. Talking things over with a personal counsellor can reduce the amount of stress that you experience, and lead to the eventual resolution of the problem.

3.4 Students' Council

The Students' Council is often a large and very important organization. It is involved in many operations, including orientation activities, tutoring services, clubs, social events, and speaker programs; it also plays an important role on elected bodies such as the Board of Governors and Senate. There are many positions available on Students' Council for those with political, business or social interests.

3.5 Chaplains' Office

Many campuses employ full-time representatives of religious organizations. They often provide a full programe of events, services, and pastoral care for the campus community.

3.6 International Students' Office

This office is sometimes an integral part of Counselling Services or it may be an autonomous unit on campus. For any international student, it is an essential service, providing a wide array of services related to immigration, visas, finances, and other personal concerns.

APPENDIX

GUIDE TO INSTRUCTORS AND COUNSELLORS

Throughout this book, we have introduced both learning strategies and ways in which students can develop their awareness of strategy use. Some of these strategies *entail setting and managing an environment* that is conducive to good studying whereas others are *cognitive strategies to engage the mind* more effectively in understanding a certain topic.

The emphasis on a student's ability to monitor his/her own strategy use reflects recent findings on *metacognition* as an important component in the learning process. This term includes both knowledge of one's own learning as well as an ability to regulate it. Metacognition is the newer emphasis in the book, and there is still debate about when and how students can acquire this kind of knowledge. This book suggests that teaching a specific strategy, a traditional practice in education, has to be accompanied by an explanation of how and when such a strategy is appropriate.

Encouraging students to make metacognitive decisions can certainly produce a diversity of student responses that may be difficult to handle in a large class. However, if learners are to gain a measure of autonomy, which then permits them to choose strategies that help them to adapt to new situations, courses, and assignments, then this is what we are advocating. You will have already noticed that capable students do come up with differing ideas. As an instructor, you might see if they suggest useful strategies that could be presented to other students in your classes.

In practice, those schools that are building learning skills into the curriculum have found that:

a) it is desireable to introduce strategies or skills that have been commonly agreed upon by a group of staff members.

b) instruction on learning skills should be organized to teach one strategy at a time. This can be reinforced in several classes.

c) such new information is better presented by subject instructors who can use relevant and interesting examples that are intrinsic to the subject content. This is preferable to introducing learning skills as an adjunct activity or in a special class.

d) credit has to be given in testing for a student's ability to demonstrate knowledge of the process as well as the product of the learning task. For example, the decision steps of a science problem (as described in Chapter 7:   SCIENCE PROBLEM SOLVING) are as important as the computations themselves.

It has also been observed that the introduction of learning skills takes some time away from content teaching and therefore is not always easy to "sell" to students. Some students do not attribute success to this kind of effort and are loathe to do "extra" work that requires such attention to process. There are a few ideas that may involve students more actively in strategy development.

1. *The Coaching Analogy*

Certain students who play or watch sports will identify with the idea of being trained to perform better through special coaching. They can recognize the value of specific practice, regular workouts, and acquiring the knowledge necessary to develop certain skills. Unfortunately, it is much harder to show them a good thinker than a good athlete, but the comparison can be made.

2. *Case Studies*

The notion that a change in approach will be useful can be highlighted more easily through specific examples such as case studies. Examples of typical case studies are at the end of certain chapters in this book. Students are often prepared to make comments on the strategies of others more readily than to comment on their own situation. Questioning that redirects the issue to the students' experiences can be an effective way of raising their awareness. Additonal examples of case studies are given in the following worksheets. You will be able to devise others that illustrate the problems you can see in your classroom.

3. *Exploration of Student Approaches*

Rather than presenting learning strategies as a list of "tips" or a series of "do's and don'ts", it is useful to investigate reasons why certain strategies work or do not work. This often means asking students about their rationale for the strategies they use to see how they can be adapted rather than replaced.

An example is students' use of highlighting while reading texts. Rather than telling them not to highlight on first reading, ask them what they are trying to achieve in that initial reading. If their goal is understanding, then it is too early to be making judgments about what is important until a complete section (this need only be a page or so) has been covered. At this point, highlighting might be very useful, while rereading, to select what is important to remember.

There are several inventories throughout the book which are designed to help with a student's personal assessment. Again, these can be adapted for your students.

4. *A Variety of Examples for Practice*

Creative use of small group discussion on different ways to apply a strategy will help to establish the idea more clearly in the repertoire of the student. The applications should not involve too much complexity at the outset as it appears to take considerable practice to learn how to apply a strategy in just one setting. Even after it has been established, the ways in which students generalize a strategy across tasks may vary tremendously.

5. *Modelling Learning Behaviour*

One challenge of this process of teaching learning skills is that often you, as the instructor, have to reconsider your own learning style and strategy. Being able to model yourself as a learner to students, both in terms of how you do things efficiently as well as what you have difficulty with, can affect your students' willingness to persist. They will then be sharing in the excitement of finding more successful ways to learn.

6. *Evaluation*

In order to encourage students to become more aware of monitoring how and when to use strategies, accurate feedback about what is successful is very important. Rewards may be fairly long term in the case of specific strategies, for example, a student who regularly reviews class notes over a whole year may very well find a positive improvement in the final course grade. However, unless some interim benefits are recognized by the student, this useful strategy may not be consistently applied.

Sample Worksheet 1

Personality Influences in Time Management

Most of us enjoy advantages and suffer disadvantages as a result of our choices about how to spend time on certain tasks. Can you identify some of these advantages and disadvantages in each of the following cases?

		Advantages	*Disadvantages*
1.	Joe accomplishes study tasks systematically. He does not take short cuts and makes decisions slowly		
2.	Nadia hurries through most assignments. She may miss details, but can do a lot in a short time.		
3.	Eric is very painstaking and never needs to redo assignments. He often overplans and fails to meet deadlines.		
4.	Ramona helps others, often in preference to completing her own work. She consults others frequently before getting down "to it".		
5.	Now, describe and assess your style in the same way.		

Sample Worksheet 2

PROBLEMS CONCENTRATING?

1. Mo is in residence and he finds that there are always interesting activities going on. This tends to distract him when he tries to settle down to work. *How can he sort out this problem?*

2. Janice wants to get into the Business School, so she settles down to work every evening after supper. She finds that she gets very fidgety after an hour. *How can she change this?*

3. When Tony reads his sociology text, he soon finds himself daydreaming. *What suggestions can you make?*

4. Patty has two brothers and a sister who all went to university, got degrees, and have good jobs. Everyone assumes Patty will do the same. She doesn't want to disappoint them, but finds it really difficult to concentrate on studying. *What kinds of things ought she to check out?*

Sample Worksheet 3

Nancy is looking very upset. She has had her results back from the first set of mid-term exams, and they are not what she expected. They are not the kind of results that she is used to.

In Grade 13, she worked really hard and won an Ontario Scholarship. She has been working hard since she came to university. In residence, she sees that many students put in fewer hours studying than she does.

Business School is her goal and she is taking courses in Business, Psychology, Sociology, Economics, and Math. The Bus. cases take hours to prepare properly. The amount of reading in Psych., Soc., and Eco. seems overwhelming, and now her marks are also sliding.

She studied for hours for the mid-terms and her marks on the multiple-choice exams for Psych., Soc., and Eco. were all in the high 60s, nowhere near her goal. And to top it all, her roommate got higher marks on two of those exams and she didn't put as much time into her studying.

Nancy is determined to find out what went wrong and to try to change things, but she is also beginning to question whether or not she's **bright** enough to make it.

QUESTIONS

1. What are the problems facing Nancy?

2. What can she do to improve her situation?

To the owner of this book:

We are interested in your reaction to *Learning for Success: Skills and Strategies for Canadian Students*, by Joan Fleet, Fiona Goodchild, and Richard Zajchowski.

1. What was your reason for using this book?

_____ university course   _____ continuing education course
_____ college course   _____ personal interest
                                 _____ other (specify)

2. In which school are you enrolled? _____.

3. Approximately how much of the book did you use?
_____ 1/4   _____ 1/2   _____ 3/4   _____ all

4. What is the best aspect of the book?

5. Have you any suggestions for improvement?

6. Is there anything that should be added?

Fold   here
